RESOURCE ROOM
CHURCH HOUSE
9 THE CLOSE
WINCHESTER
SO23 9LS
Tel: 01962 844644

KT-224-015

SIGNS OF LIFE

how goes the decade of evangelism

WINCHESTER SCHOOL OF MISSION

07210

CHURCH HOUSE PUBLISHING

ISBN 0 7151 5534 2

Published 1996 for the Board of Mission of the General Synod of the
Church of England by Church House Publishing

© The Central Board of Finance of the Church of England

All rights reserved. No part of this publication may be reproduced or
stored or transmitted by any means or in any form, electronic or
mechanical, including photocopying, recording, or any information
storage and retrieval system, without written permission which should
be sought from the Copyright Administrator, Central Board of
Finance of the Church of England, Church House, Great Smith
Street, London SW1P 3NZ.

Cover design by Julian Smith

Printed in England by Bourne Press Ltd

Contents

Preface   iv

Introduction   1

1   Defining the Decade and evangelism   3

2   Reporting action in the Decade of Evangelism   10

3   Assessing the impact of the Decade so far   42

4   Assessing the 1994 national initiatives   50

5   Identifying trends in society   53

6   Identifying enriching trends in evangelism   64

7   Developing the second half of the Decade   78

Appendix: Defining terms in evangelisation   90

Preface

Midway through the Decade of Evangelism, the Anglican Communion has asked each of its Provinces to review the way in which the Decade is being approached. Canon Robert Warren, on behalf of the Board of Mission, was asked to undertake this task for the Church of England. *Signs of Life* is the result of his review.

This report shows there are plenty of signs of life in both the Decade of Evangelism and the Church of England. More than that, it gives some helpful pointers as to how what is happening in the realm of evangelism is changing and can be developed. It gives some signs as to how to enhance the life and mission of the Church.

The various 'questions churches are asking' sections represents a built-in study guide which many churches could find a most helpful, challenging and practical way of assessing their own engagement in the work of evangelism.

So there is plenty here to enable the Church, despite the challenges it has faced in the first half of the decade, to take heart. There is also, and perhaps more importantly, much here that we need to take to heart so that the second half of the decade may build upon the striking range of initiatives that have marked the first half.

+ Thomas Leicester

Chairman, Board of Mission

Introduction

The Decade of Evangelism has been described, by Bishop Rowan Williams, as 'a necessary idiocy'. 'Necessary', because much of Western Christianity has gone to sleep on the job. 'Idiocy', because evangelism is so much the essence of the church that a decade of evangelism is rather like declaring a 'decade of breathing'.

The commitment to engage in a decade of evangelism is shared with all the mainline denominations in the United Kingdom together with 'new churches', independent churches and para-church organisations. Such a step was a bold move, representing one of very few occasions when, not just the Church of England, or even the whole Anglican Communion, but the church world-wide, has sought consciously to do a specific piece of work together over a sustained period.

In 1993 the Anglican Consultative Council called for each province to produce a mid-term decade audit. The Standing Committee of General Synod commissioned the Board of Mission to produce such an audit. In doing so, aware that it would not be possible to make additional funds or staff available for this work, the Standing Committee advised the Board to limit itself to producing simply a mid-term report. Inevitably, any audit at this stage can only be a preliminary assessment of what has been achieved.

The purpose of this report is both limited and practical. Limited, because the Board has neither the resources nor skills to produce a thorough-going audit. Practical, because it is intended to be accessible to church members in general, and Parochial Church Councils in particular, as a document to help them measure, criticise, develop and mature the efforts of the churches to tell the good news of God's revelation in Christ.

As such the report necessarily begins by defining the terms used and the limits of this report. It then moves on to reporting the wide range of activities engaged in during the first half of the Decade. This leads to a section assessing the impact of the work of the Decade in general and of the four 1994 national initiatives in particular. The identifying section of the report notes some of the major trends within society most likely to impinge on the work of evangelism and highlights some of the trends taking place in the way the church currently does evangelism. A final section on developing the second half of the Decade seeks to contribute to the way that priorities are established by local churches, dioceses, and voluntary and central agencies. Those priorities themselves relate to the goals spelt out at Lambeth 1988 and indicates ways by which they might best be taken forward in the second half of the Decade.

1

Defining the Decade and evangelism

'What is the Decade of Evangelism?' is an important question. It is under-stood, in this report, as *the commitment of the church to give particular focus to the work of evangelism in the last decade of the second Christian millennium.* The Decade, in other words, is what we the church, in response to the leadership of the bishops and, we trust, the guidance of the Holy Spirit, believe should be a particular emphasis in this decade. It is important to clarify that the Decade is, therefore, essentially a commitment by the church rather than an organisational arm of the church.

The church's concern is not the promotion of 'The Decade' as such, but rather the work of evangelism during this decade. Indeed the task is not even that of 'promoting' (in the sense of 'advertising') evange-lism. The goal rather is to communicate the faith. Making Christ Known (not the decade, or evangelism) is what the Decade of Evangelism is about and how its impact should be assessed.

The media have often struggled with such an approach. Looking for an organisation, an event, or a programme which can be reported on is very understandable, but it misses the nature of the Decade. The Decade is not an 'it', an organisation one can support, or join; nor is it 'them', something that someone else is paid to do. Rather, it is us – the whole church – living and acting in response to the Great Commission of Christ. *The Decade is us the church, putting our thought, prayer and effort into the work of evangelism.*

A second term which needs defining is that of evangelism itself. Here it is right to point out that whereas most denominations have spoken about a 'decade of evangelism', the Catholic church has consistently use the phrase 'decade of evangelisation'. Where 'evangelism' has the sharper focus expressed in the phrase 'bringing people to faith in Christ', 'evangelisation' includes the wider context of bringing the whole person, including the church and surrounding society, to the wholeness of life made available in Christ. For many these two words are summed up in the more familiar words 'evangelism' and 'mission'. However, a helpful way of distinguishing between the three concepts of mission, evangelisation and evangelism, is in the definitions

3

produced by the Revd Donald Elliott (Secretary to the Churches' Commission on Mission). They are printed as an appendix to this report (see page 90).

These two aspects can be described as the narrow-focused view and the wide-angled view of evangelism. They can easily become divorced from, and even antagonistic towards, each other. 'Evangelism' isolated from 'mission' can degenerate into a church membership drive. 'Mission', cut off from the work of sharing the faith, can become vague and lacking in gospel vitality. It is essential that they are held together. This report is written out of the conviction that mission and evangelism belong together, and seeks to hold them together in creative tension. There is a bias towards the task of communicating the faith to individuals. However, reference back to the wider task of mission, understood as participating in God's redeeming purposes and action for the whole created order, is frequently made in order to ensure that the mission/evangelism tension is held creatively.

With that background it is possible to give attention to a definition of evangelism. Books could be written in an attempt to develop a definition. A recent Board of Mission publication contained one definition for each day of the week (*Ambassador* Spring 95, issue no. 10). At a recent conference of evangelists one group exercise involved them looking at one hundred definitions of evangelism and deciding which one was most true to their experience and practice. Certainly, there is no lack of definitions. The task here is not, therefore, to develop another one, but to note the key trends in recent Anglican definitions with a view to providing sufficient definition by which to measure the work being done, and to give direction to future priorities.

The obvious starting point for an Anglican definition is the report instigated by Archbishop William Temple, entitled *Towards the Conversion of England*. This was an important report produced in 1945. Amongst it recommendations were the proposal for the church to invest in industrial mission, and in advertising. The former was done, the latter has only recently begun to happen as a result of the freeing of restrictions on religious advertising. The critics of the report point, including – at the time – J.H. Oldham, that it failed to tackle the key issue of an effective apologetic. Without a critique of the philosophy of the times there cannot be a well grounded work of evangelism. It is a point that is valid today as then.

However, in terms of developing a definition of evangelism, the report drew its definition of evangelism from the prior Archbishop's

Committee of Inquiry on the Evangelistic Work of the Church, which reported in 1918. It said:

> To evangelise is so to present Christ Jesus in the power of the Holy Spirit, that men shall come to put their trust in God through Him, to accept Him as their Saviour, and serve Him as their King in the fellowship of His Church.
> *Towards the Conversion of England*, p.1

Whilst that remains a valid definition, it was written in a very different setting from today's culture. It lacks several aspects of the church's contemporary understanding and practice of evangelism, and uses words that would not be the most natural starting point for a definition today. In particular, its use of the word 'present' can easily be taken to mean 'preach' (from a pulpit) whereas today we stress that the gospel is communicated through a range of activities and relationships, not least as a community of people who live by the values of the kingdom of God and speak of his presence in their lives. Also, not least in the light of the excesses of the 'televangelists', there is an awareness of how some evangelism can be expressed as emotional pressure and manipulation. The direct linking of 'presenting Christ' and people 'accepting Him' needs to be qualified.

More recently the joint Board of Mission and Partnership for World Mission paper, *The Measure of Mission*, (GS780A, 1987, p.38) offers the following definition:

> Evangelism is the making known of the gospel of the Lord Jesus Christ, especially to those who do not know it. . . We are charged to communicate that the life, death and resurrection of Jesus Christ is good news from God.

'Making Christ Known' points to the multi-faceted way in which that can happen. This includes visual forms such as drama, music, dance, mime and symbolic action, as well as the relational dimension of evangelism highlighted by John Finney's work in *Finding Faith Today*. By using the words 'good news' (as in *All God's Children?*, noted below), the report also highlights the awareness today that the *story* of the faith points to both the vital content of the message (Christ's life, death and resurrection), and to the way in which it is communicated (as story).

The joint Board of Education and Board of Mission report, *All God's Children?* (1992), picked up the Measure of Mission report's definition, and developed its own working definition. It is worth quoting the introductory words as well as the definition itself:

> The word 'evangelism'. . . is made up of two parts, the main part is 'evangel' (meaning good news); while the suffix 'ism' refers to procedures, actions and systems that are appropriate to the main part of the word. So evangelism means activities designed to help people discover the good news. (see pages 39-42)

Both the above reports refer to the importance of Dr. William Abraham's book, *The Logic of Evangelism,* in which he says:

> We can best improve our thinking on evangelism by conceiving it as that set of intentional activities which is governed by the goal of initiating people into the kingdom of God.
> (William Abraham, *The Logic of Evangelism,* p.95)

He amplifies the tasks of 'initiating people into the kingdom of God', by saying:

> To be initiated into the rule of God is to encounter a transcendent reality that has entered history and to find oneself drawn up into the ultimate purposes of God for history and creation.
> (William Abraham, *The Logic of Evangelism*, p.101)

Two further contemporary definitions can be added at this point. Dr Bill Burrows of Maryknoll, gives the following definition:

> Evangelisation is a process whereby God transforms human beings and enlists human help in transforming societies.
> (quoted in an address by Canon Peter Price to the USPG Council, June 1994)

Similarly, the working definition of evangelism used in the Lichfield diocese is:

> The processes by which people become disciples of Jesus Christ.

More colourfully and memorable is the definition of the Asian theologian D.T. Niles:

> Evangelism is one beggar showing another beggar where to find bread.

It is noteworthy that *process* is a key element in these definitions. This, as will be noted later, is a major development in the church's understanding of how evangelism takes place.

It is also important to note that the *end result of evangelism* is seen here not primarily in terms of church membership, but rather as participation in God's mission. That mission is understood in terms of his redeeming and liberating work in all creation until it finds fulfilment in His consummation of the Kingdom; thus weaving together the work of evangelism and mission. It is this holistic process that is shaping the church's understanding of evangelism today and on which this report is based. However, it is also important to hold onto the emphasis on *making truth known,* and on the work of evangelism as including a radical, yet unpressured, call for *a life-changing response of faith to the good news of Christ.*

A valuable tool being used by a number of diocesan missioners is the five marks of mission developed by the Anglican Consultative Council (the first four in 1984, the fifth added in 1990). It is a helpful and instructive exercise for churches to identify how they score on these various elements of mission (on a scale of 1 to 5) with a view to identifying where further action is most needed.

THE FIVE MARKS OF MISSION
as developed by the Anglican Consultative Council

1.   To proclaim the good news of the kingdom

2.   To teach, baptise and nurture new believers

3.   To respond to human need by loving service

4.   To seek to transform the unjust structures of society

5.   To strive to safeguard the integrity of creation and sustain and renew the life of the earth

---

Having given some definition of both the decade and evangelism, it is worth returning to the Lambeth Conference of 1988, which gave expression to these two aspects of mission and evangelism by not only calling for a decade of evangelism (see the quotation at the head of this report), but also called for a renewing of the missionary nature of the Church. This latter call was expressed particularly in the following recommendations:

> This Conference calls for a shift to a dynamic missionary emphasis going beyond care and nurture to proclamation and service.
> Recommendation 44, Lambeth Conference 1988.

> In many parts of the world, Anglicans have emphasised the pastoral model of ministry at the expense of mission. We believe that the Holy Spirit is now leading us to become a movement for Mission.
> *Lambeth Pastoral letter*, 7.13, p.327

This report seeks to address these two questions:

1. What progress is being made in the work of evangelism? and

2. What progress is being made in the orientation of the life of the church around God's mission in and to his world?

Before proceeding further it is worth noting that the church has been at quite different places with reference to these two sides of the Lambeth call. As far as the call to engage in evangelism was concerned, the Decade of Evangelism can be seen as an 'idea whose time has come'. As will be shown in the next section, much evangelism was taking place and would have taken place without a call to evangelism. For example, neither church planting, parish and town missions nor the development and widespread adoption of the Alpha course, are initiatives directly inspired by the Decade. However, the value of the Decade is in giving prominence and recognition to what is already being done in the area of evangelism, and in giving added impetus to these and many other initiatives.

When it comes to ordering the life of the church around mission, we find ourselves much further back in this long-term task. Here it is not so much an idea whose time has come, as a call which the church is likely to take well over a decade to heed and act upon. It is for this reason that the suggested priorities in the final section identify this aspect as needing particular attention in the second half of the Decade – without losing emphasis on the more direct work of evangelism.

QUESTIONS CHURCHES ARE ASKING

What definition of mission and evangelism best describes our approach, and how true to that understanding is our practice?

The Archbishop of Canterbury, at the Kanuga Conference (see page 32) said 'Mission which does not have evangelism as a focus is not Christian mission, and evangelism which keeps itself aloof from matters of justice and human welfare does not reflect adequately the biblical revelation.' How adequately does our approach to mission and evangelism incorporate both strands?

2

Reporting action in the Decade of Evangelism

Of one thing there can be no doubt, the Decade of Evangelism has stimulated a vast amount of action and an almost bewildering range of responses and initiatives. The problem in compiling this section has not been lack of material, but how to make sense and give some feel to the whole spectrum of action. Major and significant pieces of work will inevitably, and necessarily, have been omitted; for example, the important pastoral/evangelistic work of chaplains to higher education, hospitals, prisons and industry. The lack of reference to any particular diocese in no way indicates lack of interesting stories. All that can be told are a series of all too brief descriptions which make it clear in how many ways the church is seeking to respond to the call to evangelism, and to establish something of a sense of a mosaic of actions.

It is important to make this point for, the media in particular, have been inclined to write premature obituaries of the Decade. In large measure this is because the Decade is being worked out at the local level rather than through high-profile events. That is healthy, but it is not visible. It is likely, for example, that in 1995 more people will be involved in enquirer groups than would have happened had there been a 'Billy Graham Mission England' such as took place in 1985. However, because it is happening without that media event, the camera at least, has difficulty seeing it.

The reporting which follows simply gives a sample of initiatives taken in the first five years.

In the local church

The response of churches to the Decade has inevitably been varied. Many have taken the whole challenge seriously and sought to respond accordingly. As the mission statement of one church put it:

> We accept that the Decade of Evangelism, being an initiative of the bishops and leaders of the main Christian Churches, is a vitally important initiative for the future

health and vigour of Christianity, locally, nationally and internationally. We undertake to see this as representing both an opportunity and an obligation.

Some churches have come on board as a result of further reflection on what the Decade is about, or as a result of the arrival of a new incumbent, or through the way that the losses incurred by the Church Commissioners have 'focused the mind'. Others have yet to engage with the challenge of the Decade. Among these are churches that feel dispirited by the decision about the ordination of women, or because they feel weighed down by the quota, the buildings and 'keeping the show on the road', and yet others because evangelism seems a foreign and threatening concept.

Among the many churches that have sought to engage with the Decade, a number of responses can be identified. The Decade has been seen as a stimulus to *the development of mission statements,* five year plans and parish strategies. These are long-term commitments to give purpose and direction to the life of the church, and are identifying which things need to be given highest priority and which activities need to be scaled down or allowed to die.

For other churches the focus in the Decade has been on some *local piece of evangelistic activity,* often done in conjunction with churches of other denominations in their area. Work with young people, establishing of playgroups, parent and toddler groups, running parenting courses, setting up drop-in centres or thrift shops being just some of the initiatives taken.

In some churches the Decade has led to the development of a *parish mission.* Often these are local mission projects in which several churches in an area work together. Typically a mission is planned two years ahead. Some have tended to dismiss 'missions' as belonging to the 'old way of doing things'. If done in the 'old', that is exclusively preaching, style that would be a valid criticism, but many churches have found creative new ways of making the faith known. Presentations in pubs have been conducted by some, with other people picking up the lyrics of pop groups ('The gospel according to Queen') and relating the Christian faith to the issues raised. Clowning, videos, street theatre, after dinner speakers for local business people, and fun events for children have all found a place. Meetings in homes, typically with 'faith sharing' being done by lay members of the church, play a larger part than public meetings and pulpit addresses.

In some areas (such as Cardiff, Spalding, Dronfield, Reading, Plymouth, York, to name just a few), churches have cooperated ecumenically in arranging a mission. In York the 1,500 seater Barbican Centre was filled for a week with people coming to hear the Archbishop of York, Lord Tonypandy, Roy and Fiona Castle, and Dr Donald English. Such events usually gain wide coverage in local press and other media.

One particular initiative in many churches has been the setting up of *enquirer groups*. The positive result of this shift has yet to be felt. It means that evangelism, and the initiation of newcomers to the church and to the faith, is being built into the on-going life of the church, rather than relegated to a 'one-off' event. It necessarily also releases lay people into a variety of forms of service, since it is not possible to take this approach without considerable teamwork. As will be noted later, this is one of the major trends in the way evangelism is currently done – through groups, in the context of relationships and over a period of time – rather than in one-off situations. The Christian Publicity Organisation reports a significant trend in requests for literature for distribution in the following terms:

> Churches are changing their style of evangelism from mass tract distribution with little personal contact, to relational evangelism where only individuals who are 'known' are given literature, and literature of greater quality.

Other churches have been developing ways of building an annual mission focus into the life of the church. Rather along the lines of One World Week, churches have developed – often at the start of the autumn programme – a 'Harvest Hospitality Week', or an 'Open Doors Fortnight', in which welcome of visitors and enquirers to events designed as stepping stones into faith-enquiry and church membership forms the focus. This is a manageable and creative way for a church to give expression to evangelism. Usually enquirers groups are scheduled to start soon after such a week.

The last two expressions link with the development of stepping stones to faith, well set out in Steve Croft's book *Growing New Christians*. These include a variety of ways of enabling people to have some initial, and unthreatening, experience of church life, such as outlined under 'a piece of evangelistic activity' above. A number of churches working on this approach report that they are having to start 'further back' all the time. Some now begin with coach trips to the theatre, a seaside resort, tourist attraction or pilgrimage centre, as a necessary first step in building relationships.

For other churches the Decade has led to a more conscious engagement with the local community and local community issues. Helping to establish housing projects, rights and advice centres, street wardens, soup runs for the homeless, surveys of local needs and other activities designed to serve the people in the area. This approach to mission is well expressed in Raymond Fung's *The Isaiah Vision*, and in John Reader's *Local Theology*. They are important ways in which evangelism and social action are being creatively woven together.

Related to the above is a growing focus on faith at work, both in terms of training church members to apply their faith in the workplace, and in establishing faith networks in places of employment where Christians, ecumenically, can come together to explore and support each other in the application of their faith to the world of work. The Board of Education's six week course on *Monday Matters,* and the more recently published (by Cassells and SU) *Sunday-Monday Course,* are valuable resources for this aspect of expressing the faith.

The priority of evangelism in a growing number of churches has taken the form of church planting. This has many expressions (see the General Synod report *Breaking New Ground*). Related to this is the development of alternative expressions of worship – usually amongst young people, or with young adults. See below under 'national trends'.

A crucial way in which many churches are engaging with the Decade is not by taking on any new initiatives but simply by doing a better job. There is evidence that a more conscious mission orientation is shaping the preparation of young couples for marriage, and the handling of baptism enquiries. The Christian Enquiry Agency, Christian Publicity Organisation and the Board of Mission have co-operated to produce a series of Contact Makers leaflets for use at occasional offices and key festivals.

The 'Seeker-service' approach is just one way in which the essentially evangelistic nature of Sunday services is being addressed. An emphasis on lay training, both for work within the life of the church, and in equipping people to relate their faith to the whole of life, is also evidence of the way that the missionary nature of the church's teaching role is being expressed.

Finally, for a number of churches the primary focus of action in the Decade has been to participate not so much in any of the above as in the various diocesan and national trends and initiatives identified below.

In the dioceses

As with evangelism at the local level, when we turn our attention to what is happening in the dioceses, a striking variety and much skilful creativity are evident. The problem in reporting it has been to find out all that has been going on, and then discover some framework that can make sense of the burst of activity generated by the Decade. Some of the main contours of diocesan action can be identified under the following headings.

Strategic planning has been one area significantly shaped by the backdrop of the Decade. This has been further stimulated in the light of the need for change as a result of the losses sustained by the Church Commissioners and the consequent cut back in central funding. Many dioceses have developed a structural review and process of internal change with mission as the integrating theme. Among many such reviews are the Towards 2000 plan in the Ely and York diocese, the Renewal for Mission process of re-structuring in the Southwark diocese, New Ways for New Times, the Bishop's manifesto of the Lincoln diocese, and The Future strategy document forming the basis of work in the Canterbury diocese. Towards 2001 AD (a way forward for parish and diocese) is the mission strategy of the Leicester diocese; Developing Ministry programme is the basis of the mission and evangelism work in the Southwell diocese, Growing the Kingdom is a similar strategic document which churches are working on in the Lichfield diocese. The Wakefield diocese developed a strategic plan and communicated it very effectively throughout the diocese by means of a video *Opening the Door to Faith*; indeed later it was taken up and used in a number of other dioceses as well.

This list is only a sample. Most dioceses have developed similar strategies and projects designed to strengthen the work of mission, often in the context of re-organisation.

Many of these plans are still at the design/consultation and early implementation stage. Five dioceses are being represented at a Consultation at St George's Windsor in early 1996 where it is hoped to develop some 'best practice' models that can be made available more widely. It is being set up by the Decade of Evangelism Steering Group of the Board of Mission as part of its resourcing of structural renewal in the church.

Episcopal missions have played a significant role in a number of dioceses. Both the Bishops of Sheffield and Coventry have taken preaching/teaching missions onto (and beside!) the canals in their dioceses. The Archbishop of Canterbury has made time in his full schedule to lead a series of similar missions in the deaneries of his diocese. Many bishops, including especially suffragan bishops, have cleared their diaries to be available to lead missions, often in deaneries.

Episcopal calls to mission have been addressed to churches in a number of dioceses, with a view to inviting every parish to discern and offer its plans for forwarding the work of evangelism in its area. Liverpool and Manchester are just two such dioceses where this approach has been a major part of the total response to the Decade. One Step at a Time is a programme developed in the Salisbury diocese to enable churches to 'find out more about themselves and plan for the future through the Decade of Evangelism and beyond'. The Guildford diocese is having a major initiative in 1997 called Pilgrim's Way. Under the leadership of the bishop, the emphasis is on openness, hospitality, sharing the faith and encouraging parishes to consider the nature of the life of the church.

Other episcopal initiatives have involved bishops being at the forefront of teaching and training programmes, and of three and five year programmes which hold together the various strands of the church around the focus of the Decade. The Bishop of Ripon's 'bishop's initiatives for the decade' (called *Striking Gospel Gold*) has three elements: devotion (going to church), formation (growing in faith) and action (power for living). This is seen as a spiral in which the church is to make progress in, and continually return to and be renewed in, each of these elements. The Bishop of Bath and Wells has instituted a programme entitled Go for God. It began with a year of prayer, has included 'Bishop's mission visitors' going to virtually every parish to listen to their vision, hopes and needs in the area of mission. The first two stages will then be followed by a focus on mission action in the second half of the Decade.

There is little doubt that the Decade has made most headway in dioceses where the bishop has taken a clear and visible lead.

Diocesan mission structures, have been developed in many dioceses during the Decade to ensure that the work of mission is forwarded in an on-going way. The diocese of Peterborough, for example, has established a Council for Evangelism which has provided a whole series of ideas. The diocese of Southwark has appointed six incumbents as 'archdeaconry advisers in evangelism', who work with the Canon Missioner and with others in the three episcopal area mission teams, each working with an area bishop.

15

Diocesan mission events have taken place around the country. God in the Parks was a series of open air events, ecumenically run and making use of well known evangelists, around the parks of Bradford. It drew hundreds of people to evangelistic events from across the diocese. Time Travelling! was a fine, and very thoroughly researched and resourced pilgrimage for school children to Southwell Minster. It was linked with schools and the national curriculum (for which lesson materials were provided). It was spoken of highly by educationalists in the area and attracted over 4,000 children into a pilgrimage experience which did much to make the Christian faith a reality to them. It could well provide a model for other dioceses, cathedrals and centres of pilgrimage. On similar lines, the Lincoln diocese has held Church School Festivals in the Cathedral for a number of years.

Focus on training has been a mark of the opening years of the Decade with several dioceses reporting a striking level of attendance (over 2,000 in the Southwell diocese at an all-ages training event). The Wakefield diocese had to turn people away from an over-subscribed day on Growing New Christians. The Blackburn diocese has developed 'schools of evangelism' out of its prior experience of running 'schools of prayer'. The Lichfield diocese, likewise, has been running training in evangelism courses for several years for over six hundred people each year. It is clear that an eagerness for training is one of the distinguishing marks of the Decade to date. The way in which a great variety of training events are being attended suggests an underlying health in the church's attitude towards mission.

One example of this emphasis is the work in the Manchester diocese in developing an eighteen session course entitled *More Effective Witness*. The emphasis is on witness in a secular world.

Prayer and spirituality have also been evident in a number of dioceses, with prayer schools, prayer missions, prayer walking (walking and praying for an area), all taking place around the country. In addition to what is reported above about the diocese of Bath and Wells, the emphasis on prayer has also marked the work done in the Blackburn diocese. The Gloucester diocese has developed a creative prayer initiative called King Pin (standing for Kingdom Prayer Initiative Network). It has a quarterly newsheet, and is focused on praying for ecumenical evangelistic work in its widest sense. By using the network approach it probably also engages with those who are reluctant meeting-attenders. Spirituality courses are also being developed in the Southwark and Guildford dioceses, to name just two, doubtless of many.

In view of what is said about the priority of spirituality later in this report, this represents a key area of development in the Decade.

Pilgrimage has played an important part in expressing the church's concern to be among people and to relate to its roots. The 1997 Pilgrimages are simply a development of this revival of interest in pilgrimage. The March for Jesus events, and the various Walks of a Thousand Men, etc., show how – with creative interpretation – the old practices of pilgrimage are finding new expression.

Encouraging the work of evangelists. A number of dioceses have paid particular attention to the recognition, training, deployment and support of evangelists. In the Rochester diocese, under Bishop Michael Turnbull, a major training programme for local evangelists was established. The training takes two years, leads to diocesan accreditation, and results in people with varied evangelistic gifts being deployed in a range of different ways. They form part of the diocesan fellowship of evangelists who meet three times a year for mutual support and in-service training. The dioceses of Guildford, Lichfield and Sheffield (the latter in conjunction with the Church Army Training College in the city) are also developing the training of evangelists. The Peterborough diocese developed the idea of Lay Evangelists. The idea began in one parish, was then used in a deanery mission and is now close to being a diocesan-wide enterprise. A parallel project has been jointly organised by the Church Army, Northern Baptist College and Oasis Trust. It includes both residential and distance learning. The scheme is now validated by the University of Leeds.

Appointing mission officers. One of the most significant outcomes of the Lambeth call for a Decade of Evangelism has been the growth in the number of appointments in mission and evangelism. They are playing an important role in helping churches to reflect upon, develop and do the work of evangelism. They are often closely involved with the bishop and with the development of a diocesan strategy for mission and evangelism. They have stimulated, encouraged and facilitated much of the work already outlined. They have formed an effective network for the exchange of information and ideas.

Writing about evangelism before Lambeth 1988, Max Warren could speak of a 'measure of bewilderment' as to how to set about evangelism. Although contemporary culture presents the confusion of a sometimes hostile world in which to work, missioners have done important work in developing, alongside local churches, workable schemes and ideas which are now much more plentiful. It is right that the church acknowledges the significant contributions of such sector ministries.

Breaking church growth barriers is an important issue that some dioceses have been giving attention to in the Decade. There is clear statistical evidence that churches grow towards an invisible limiting size (around 150), and then continually bounce off that limit (the 'glass ceiling' effect). Wakefield, York and Sheffield dioceses in particular have been addressing this important issue in seeking to help churches find their way through.

Providing consultants to help develop evangelism and the whole renewal of the life of the church, has been a further way in which dioceses have responded to the Decade. The York diocese has commissioned twelve advisers in evangelism for just this purpose. Most of the team are in full-time work (including a rural dean and a headteacher). Their task is to forward the work of evangelism, by a variety of means, under the leadership of the diocesan evangelist.

A number of dioceses have also put their energies, not so much into the items listed in this section, but into some of the things mentioned in the previous section on mission through the local church, and in the following two sections.

Nationally

Several things stand out at this level. First is the series of national initiatives which took place in the first part of 1994. The four projects were the Council of Churches for Britain and Ireland's (CCBI) Lent course entitled Have Another Look. It was designed to be run in such a way that friends, neighbours and enquirers about the faith could feel at home in the study groups. On Fire! was an inter-church initiative which gave an overall structure to public celebratory events, timed for Pentecost, but left much freedom for local adaptation and creativity too. The Minus to Plus project was mounted by Reinhard Bonke (of the Christ for all Nations organisation), a German Pentecostal pastor who works largely in Africa. The aim was to distribute a gospel booklet (called *Minus to Plus*) to every home in England. The final initiative was mounted by the Pentecostal churches in England. It was called the JIM (Jesus In Me) campaign.

In view of the scale and visibility of these four projects a separate section is included in an attempt to assess the level of impact and value of these major events (see pages 50-2).

Second is the work of Springboard, an initiative of the Archbishops of Canterbury and York to further the work of evangelism in the course of the decade. The team consists of Bishop Michael Marshall, Canon Michael Green, Mrs Rosemary Green, and Martin Cavender (the administrator). The work of Springboard is being reviewed separately, and a second phase of their work is about to be launched. However, a brief comment on the work of Springboard is in order here.

Amongst the particular contributions of Springboard to the work of the Decade so far, the following can be listed. They quickly identified the close link between evangelism, apologetics and spirituality. This is an important insight that the church needs to hold on to as it turns its attention to the second half of the Decade. They have been a source of inspiration for many in the varied places they have visited, bringing an urgency to proclaim Christ, and stimulating reflection on what the Christian faith has to say to today's world. The small team has generated a considerable writing output made available to the whole church. They have given the Decade a public face and visibility wherever they have gone. Their travelling schools around dioceses have been well received, although they would be the first to recognise that they have been on a steep learning curve as they have tried to relate well to a wide range of contrasting situations.

Diocesan missioners report many positive fruits from visits by Springboard, including a sense of hope, and a renewal of confidence and enthusiasm about the gospel and the relevance of the Christian faith to the modern world.

It is right to express the church's appreciation for this initiative by the Archbishops, and for the willingness of the team to work to such a stretching schedule over a sustained period. Few can know how draining it is to sleep over two hundred nights a year somewhere other than home, and to be constantly on the move from one unique group to another.

Third is advertising. This was one of the things that *Towards the Conversion of England* urged the church to engage with – though little was actually done at the time. However, since the relaxation of the ban on religious groups advertising on commercially-funded radio and television was relaxed in 1991, the Churches Advertising Network has mounted a number of campaigns, mainly at Christmas and Easter, using radio, billboards, posters and cards to encourage people to attend church. This has complemented the work of the Churches Enquiry Agency with its advertisements in the press which have attracted the interest, in the main, of young men in the 18 to 30 years age group.

The growing number of training courses in communications skills organised by the Communications Department of General Synod is helping church members to develop confidence in communicating their faith using mass means of communication.

The Communication Department's handbook, *How to Promote your Church,* is a valuable resource that helps a church to look at the many ways – for better or for worse – that it does communicate about itself and the Christian faith. Any church making use of it would find significant help in improving how it communicates with the surrounding community. Several dioceses have made copies available to every church. It is likely to prove a wise investment.

Fourth, it is appropriate to record here two major initiatives that are scheduled for the remaining years, as far as nationally co-ordinated events are concerned. In 1997 two pilgrimages, marking the death of St Columba and the arrival of St Augustine, will take place and draw in many churches and dioceses along the routes planned. In 1999 the church, and indeed the whole of our national society, will be celebrating the millennium. A steering group has already been set up by the Archbishop of Canterbury to help in the co-ordination of the church's contribution to those celebrations. That is likely to be, not least, in reminding all involved of who is the true focus of the millennium's celebration.

Through *Faith in the City* and *Faith in the Countryside*

This report began by suggesting that the Decade of Evangelism was one of those rare occasions where the churches in general, and the Church of England in particular, have sought to do a specific piece of work. The two major reports *Faith in the City* and *Faith in the Countryside* have several connections with the Decade of Evangelism. Their concern was to forward the church's mission in two contrasting areas of national life. They also both constituted occasions when the Church of England, as in the Decade, sought to focus, develop and resource its mission over a sustained period. It is important, therefore, to reflect on the impact of the Decade in those two areas and on the ways in which those working to follow-up such reports have sought to relate the concerns of the Decade with the work already established through these respective reports.

Faith in the City

It is not easy to assess the effect of the Decade on Urban Priority Areas. There may not be an explicit effect, but it is clear that the emphasis of the Decade has affected congregations and spilt over into what is being said within the Bishops' Advisory Group for Urban Priority Areas (BAGUPA) network. The whole issue of the church making a shift to missionary mode is very relevant to UPAs. There are good models of mission in UPAs that are relevant to the rest of the church, though some UPA parishes feel dispirited and burdened by the pressure of vandalism, family breakdown and unemployment.

However, there is a growing confidence in some UPAs to speak about faith and to relate faith to action in the community. There is a shift from seeing priests as people who care for the hurting in the community to seeking priests as missionary leaders who enable congregations to be both pastoral and missionary. In some dioceses, such as Birmingham and Chelmsford, it is in UPAs that some of the fastest growing churches in the diocese can be found. There is a spirit of generosity often to be found in UPAs because people know their need of God and give generously because they are genuinely thankful.

The Link Officers' Conference has looked at faith in action – prophecy, partnership, community development, community ministry organising and service.

Faith in the Countryside

Evangelism in rural areas is being expressed in the context of several major issues.

One such issue is the increasing scarcity of full-time clergy. This means that a growing amount of church life, including engagement with and witness to, the local community is being conducted by church members. Another factor is that evangelism can have negative confrontation implications in rural communities where people know each other well.

In rural areas the church building, as a centre for pilgrimage and tourism (and people making the journey from tourism to pilgrimage) often plays a major part. It is also crucial as a place of celebration through the occasional offices. Local church as bridge-builder is often the best model for engaging with and witnessing to a rural community. A rural evangelism video, *Hidden Treasure,* has just been produced. The development of the *Country Way* magazine for the rural Church has also been a significant help in the cross-fertilising of good ideas between rural churches. As with the situation in UPAs, it has also to be acknowledged that some rural churches feel neglected, weighed down by maintaining buildings, and bereft of more ready access to 'their' vicar when they are part of a multi-benefice parish.

Among young people

One of the major areas where the work of evangelism is finding new and creative contemporary expression is among young people and those seeking to communicate the Christian faith to the youth culture. Aware of this spontaneous expression of new forms of evangelism, the Archbishop of Canterbury, in 1994, appointed Pete Ward to be his advisor in youth work. Pete Ward had been involved in Oxford Youth Works, an outreach project which is also involved in training youth workers, and continues to be involved in that work part-time. He has identified the following four signs of new life in the work of evangelism among young people, which is obviously a vital part of the church's future.

First, there are some signs that church based youth work is finding fruitful new expression. There is growth, in some places, of church based youth work, especially where churches have appointed full-time youth workers. Often the signs of growth are associated with new expressions of this type of youth work. Evidence of this can be seen in the work of the Worldwide Message Tribe, a band which goes around schools playing and communicating the Christian faith. A similar work of the Malachi Community Trust, based in Birmingham, also has developed a schools work, using music, drama and dance alongside structured class work to address the issues faced by the pressures of modern life on young people. Holy Disorder, based in the Gloucester diocese, has spread rapidly in the first two years of its existence. So also have groups which relate to Soul Survivor, the National Youth Conference and network based on St Andrew's Church Chorleywood, in the St Albans diocese. All these operations are essentially working from the inside out, starting with young people involved in church life.

Second, a whole new generation of people are emerging with a visionary commitment to 'incarnational relationship-based outreach'. At a recent consultation set up by Pete Ward, over sixty people from all over the country, many from Anglican churches, were present. They are deeply committed to the long-term work of building relationships, working with a contextualised understanding of the gospel ('The Eternal Word speaks only in the voice of local dialects') and a

22

commitment to develop alternative expressions of worship. For example, one group in Hull is exploring the implications of a simple lifestyle and of community living. The project is partly funded by the Church Urban Fund. Youth for Christ has half a dozen projects of a similar nature which it is exploring and supporting. These projects are working from the outside in, taking their starting point from engagement with young people who have no church connections.

Third, much of the new life and energy is based around worship and spirituality. This is true both for young people themselves and for their leaders. The old dichotomy between charismatic worship and commitment to urban ministry seems to be disappearing. What is emerging is a missionary *and* servant engagement with young people which is addressing the complex and often destructive forces around young people today, that is energised by encounter with God in worship and spirituality. It is giving a new energy to evangelism, and a more holistic practice.

Fourth, the Archbishop's appointment of an advisor in youth work was designed to stimulate, and integrate, the variety of ways of practising relational outreach. As a result much has been achieved by way of linking people working on otherwise unrelated and unsupported projects. This has facilitated considerable cross-fertilising of ideas, a growth in the sense of being part of a bigger movement, and the maturing of the theological base of the whole movement. Pete Ward in particular has been heavily involved in contacting people doing this type of work, building networks, contributing ideas, and generating the writing of books such as *Relational Youth Work* (Lynx, 1995) and the companion *Church and Youth Ministry* (Lynx, 1995), both edited by Pete Ward.

There is a need for churches, working from the inside out to be encouraged in what they are doing. However, those involved in working from the outside in find themselves in a more vulnerable, less easily understood, yet arguably more vital role. Certainly, the vast majority of young people are now outside the life of local churches.

It would seem vital for there to be a concentration of resources, learning and expertise and the mobilising of volunteers to do this work. The shape of such projects which are emerging have the following characteristics:

* *evangelistic work* with unchurched young people

* centres for *training* of a practical on-the-job nature for volunteer workers

* *holistic* approach which addresses the whole person in their context

* *incarnational* engagement with particular cultural settings

* *contextualised worship and spirituality* arising from the young people

* *self-propagating projects* which can reproduce and multiply themselves

---

QUESTIONS CHURCHES ARE ASKING

Do we have a calling or opportunity to be engaged in, or give support to, such a project?

Are we willing to take the risks and face the costs of providing buildings and staffing for such a project?

Through black Anglicans

The Black Anglican Celebration for the Decade of Evangelism was held in York University in July 1994, and is reported on in *Roots and Wings*. This Celebration was part of the long struggle for recognition of the part that Black Anglicans play in the Church of England. The story of this process is recounted in the report, *Seeds of Hope* (published in 1991).

The Celebration was organised by the General Synod's Committee on Black Anglican Concerns (CBAC) which, a few months before the Celebration, had produced the report *How We Stand*. That report showed something of the scale of the contribution of black people to the life of the Church of England. Twenty seven thousand black Anglicans worship each week in churches covering every diocese in England. Strikingly they bring a significantly higher proportion of children with them than the rest of the church – over six children coming with every ten black Anglicans, compared with less than three with the rest of the worshipping community. The black community within the Church of England is a youthful one.

The Celebration itself was clearly a joyful, thoughtful and striking experience. Over three hundred people attended, with both archbishops present, plus twenty diocesan bishops and representatives from every diocese. Two thirds of those attending were black, with an equal balance between the sexes, lay participation far greater than the clerical, and with a bias towards the younger end of the age range. The worship was not only vibrant, but strikingly varied and creative, with – for example – the opening worship including Indian and Chinese dance and a black gospel singer. In a subsequent meeting of General Synod a sample of this worship was used to begin one day's session. It made clear to all present just how rich and varied Anglican worship is today.

The Celebration made evident many of the significant contributions which black Anglicans are making to the life of the church. Among them are the following, each of which point, significantly, to some aspect of integration of evangelism with the whole of the life of the Christian church.

Evangelism and worship. Black Anglicans witness to the cultural diversity and great creativity which is all too easily suppressed and locked away yet is available for the enriching of worship and the communication of the gospel. Black Anglicans have the ability to express faith in worship in a way that communicates to people from a variety of cultural backgrounds. This very fact also highlights the need for the Church to find ways of expressing faith in worship that communicates with the mosaic of cultures and groupings which increasingly characterise modern society.

Evangelism and young people. The black Anglican community not only has a more youthful profile than the rest of the church, it also has highly committed young people who have the ability to communicate their faith with their contemporaries. That high level of commitment is itself a reflection of the commitment of the older generation who form the backbone of the black Anglican community. This gifting not only needs to be harnessed, but is also seen as a model for how the rest of the Church should do the work of evangelism. However, the Church must recognise that these young people are likely to be the quickest to spot discrimination and injustice within the church, and the least likely to remain patient or passive. Failure to recognise them and their contribution could all too easily lose them and what they have to offer.

Evangelism and spirituality. Black Anglicans reflect as wide a range of church traditions as the rest of Anglicans. However, there is a strong spirituality at the heart of this grouping within the Church which is refreshing and attractive. In view of what is said later in this report about the trend towards spirituality as the way in which the gospel is communicated today, it is likely that the rest of the church has much to learn, and catch, from black Anglicans at this point.

Evangelism and dialogue in the inter-faith context. Often having roots in a multi-faith context, and from having themselves experienced suspicion and being marginalising, many black Anglicans have a rich and sensitive contribution to make in the area of relating to, working in partnership with, and practising authentic witness among, those of other faith communities.

Evangelism and justice. The presence of black Anglicans in the Church of England constitutes a call to justice within the church. 'The church can only tackle racism effectively in the wider society if first of all it is prepared to tackle racism within its own institutions' (*Seeds of Hope*, p.1). It also points to one vital way in which the work of the gospel is to be advanced; namely by the practice of the gospel of reconciliation within the life of the church. Certainly the leadership of black Anglicans, not least through CBAC, is committed to reconciliation and the celebration of the inclusive and diverse nature of the Anglican Communion. It is vital that this finds an echoing response in the whole church so that the good news of God's reconciling love may not only be preached but practised by the church.

QUESTIONS CHURCHES ARE ASKING

How welcoming is our church to people from a variety of racial backgrounds?

In the light of the particular contributions, identified above, which black Anglicans are making to the church, how well is our church drawing on those particular strengths?

By women

The contribution of women to the work of evangelism is immense, though often unnoticed. The number of women engaged in pulpit evangelism is small. Their contribution is more often through relationships. Typically women have a less visible role in evangelism. One possible explanation of the reason why there are more women than men in most churches, is that women have done a better job at evangelising other women then men have done in evangelising men. Christian women who are mothers are often primary evangelists who pass on their faith to their children and within the family. This is true in many cultures.

The decision of General Synod to ordain women to the priesthood occurred in the first half of the Decade of Evangelism. Many people saw the ordination of women as a key to the mission of the church. Questions had been asked about whether, if the Church could not model equality and inclusiveness in its ministry, it could preach about the inclusive nature of the gospel with integrity. Others saw the ordination of women to the priesthood as impairing the catholicity of the church and so damaging the nature and mission of the Church of England. Appeal was made to the indivisible relationship between unity, mission and evangelism. In the present setting it does seem as if both these arguments are shaping the church's engagement in evangelism. However, it does appear that where women priests have been involved in leading churches, there is evidence of a more relational and nurturing approach to church life, and to evangelism. It seems to be having a positive effect.

The Decade of Evangelism has largely overlapped with the Ecumenical Decade in Solidarity with Women. The Ecumenical Decade was launched in 1988 at the instigation of the World Council of Churches and in Britain it had its launch at Easter 1988. The aims of the Decade are to empower, affirm and give visibility to, enable and encourage women in the churches and in the world. The existence of the Decade of Evangelism has not made it easy to feature the Ecumenical Decade in Solidarity with Women in the life of the church with any great success or prominence. In some minds the two may be confused and in others there may be an unhelpful sense of competition with a fear that either agenda may be obscured by the other.

All of the work in the Ecumenical Decade has a mission and evangelistic component. For many women the fact that the Church (or a small part of it at least) is considering the issues that affect them every day (such as violence, pornography, low pay, etc) is an important part of our mission. The Church still has a long way to go in this area. The ordination of women has gone some way towards this, but much remains to be done. The work of the Ecumenical Decade is healing some of the deep wounds that the Church, among others, has inflicted on women in our society. By paying attention to these issues, the Church is showing the love of Christ. The idea that the church's engagement with women's issues is a distraction from the real work of evangelism is wide of the mark, and reveals a misunderstanding of the whole mission of the Church. Issues concerning women are not tangential to the gospel but are a part of its whole message of transforming and affirming love.

QUESTIONS CHURCHES ARE ASKING

Where are women in our church already doing the work of evangelism and how can we recognise and support them?

How can we encourage women to engage more fully in the work of evangelism?

Ecumenically

An important aspect of the launching and first half of the Decade of Evangelism has been the extent to which it has happened ecumenically.

Fascinatingly the origins of the idea of a Decade of Evangelism are shrouded in mystery. It seems to have start spontaneously in a number of different places at around the same time. For example, the Pope mentioned the idea in a letter to Canadians a few weeks before Lambeth 1988. It is wise for the churches to celebrate this mystery and not seek ownership of the idea for any one denomination. In the Anglican communion it was proposed and taken up by Lambeth 1988, and then supported by General Synod in 1989. Virtually all Christian denominations and groupings are involved. Free Churches acknowledge that the decision of the Church of England to become involved was a great stimulus to their positive response, as was the Papal commitment to a Decade of Evangelisation.

Through Churches Together in England (CTE) a co-ordinating Group For Evangelisation (GFE), composed largely of those with responsibilities for evangelism within their denomination or agency, was set up. The Group is chaired by Canon Philip King, secretary of the Board of Mission, and serviced by a part-time secretary and URC minister, the Revd Roger Whitehead. That Group has sought to stimulate co-operation and cross-fertilisation of ideas and practice, as well as to co-ordinate central initiatives. It played a central role in the Have Another Look Lent project, and On Fire! Joint evangelism, it is important to remember, was seen as one of the objectives of the new Ecumenical Instruments which were launched in the autumn of 1990. Indeed the first co-ordinating group set up by CTE was the GFE.

The Churches Commission on Mission (CCOM) of the Council of Churches for Britain and Ireland (CCBI), has played an important part in furthering the work of evangelism ecumenically. It is the group which includes representatives of all the voluntary societies working overseas, and where the Church of England co-operates with other churches on overseas work. It is also an important forum for the Churches as they address mission issues 'at home'; where 'home' includes Ireland, Wales and Scotland.

The Churches Commission on Mission has set up a 'missionary congregations learning project', which works ecumenically. One of the particular concerns of this project is the discovery of ways of the Church operating, in the Decade of Evangelism, which will result in a permanent shift in orientation to mission well beyond the Decade. Similar work in this area is being done by Canon Robert Warren on behalf of the Board of Mission, as well as parallel work by the Revd Dr David Spriggs of the Evangelical Alliance. They keep in regular contact with each other's work and seek to make the learning experience a joint one at every stage. The GFE has not only done valuable work of co-ordination and co-operation, but also testifies to a significant change of mood. As Roger Whitehead puts it:

> All Churches now need to acknowledge that the task is beyond any one of us: the Decade is one of the 'new alliances' in which evangelism has become a unifying and not dividing factor.

At the local level, it can now be said that missions are normally organised ecumenically. Even where a single church initiates and runs a mission, partnership is sought with other churches. More typically, plans are initiated and developed in a mutual partnership of many churches. This is particularly true of town and city-wide missions.

One of the, perhaps unexpected, side effects of the Decade could be the experiencing of a truth that many have argued for over the years, namely that we find our unity most fruitfully not so much by seeking unity as an end in itself, but *as we engage in mission together*. Whilst this is likely to be welcomed by many, the churches will need to be prepared for the fact that 'new alliances' as well as deepening partner-

29

ship may require significant changes in existing denominational structures.

In the area of inter-faith

The initial impact of the Decade of Evangelism seemed to have a negative effect in the delicate area of inter-faith relations. Other faith communities felt a sense of threat, and feared that they were going to be particularly 'targeted' during this period. The Jewish 'decade of renewal' and the Muslim 'decade of revival' were immediately announced but nothing has been heard of them since.

However, out of this initial response, good things have come. It was a considerable stimulus to the development of some important and helpful guidelines for inter-faith dialogue which have been published in the leaflet *Building Relations with People of Different Faiths and Beliefs*. Whilst some faiths do not engage in evangelism (such as Jews, etc) most do (Christians, Muslims, Buddhists, etc). This leaflet, itself the fruit of painstaking dialogue, can be seen as something of a charter for sensitive, respectful, inter-faith dialogue.

At the beginning of the Decade, the Commission for Inter-Faith Relations (a commission of the Council Churches for Britain and Ireland) published *In Good Faith* which is a guide to 'the four principles of Interfaith Dialogue'. Those four principles are:

1. Dialogue begins when people meet each other

2. Dialogue depends upon mutual understanding and mutual trust

3. Dialogue makes it possible to share in service to the community

4. Dialogue becomes the medium of authentic witness

In an increasingly plural society these principles can be seen as relevant to all evangelism. They resonate strongly with the work of Raymond Fung in *The Isaiah Vision*, about the building of a mission-orientated church through the processes of partnership, invitation to worship, and invitation to discipleship.

At this stage in the Decade there is little evidence to suggest any special 'targeting' of other faith adherents in the work of evangelism.

However, where churches are set in communities with significant other faith communities, dialogue and sensitive evangelism have been taking place. In some places returning missionaries have been leading the way in this, helping churches to set up multi-cultural and multiethnic congregations. Missionary societies have given valuable advice, support and resources to help in this work. For example, Crosslinks has produced a video called *Good Neighbours* to help those wanting to engage with people from other faiths; they are also setting up a consultancy scheme, in conjunction with the Church Pastoral Aid Society to help churches relate well to other ethnic communities within their parishes. The Church Mission Society has developed a substantial range of resources not least of which is its course on Islam entitled *The Cross and the Crescent.*

In short, the Decade, not least through the anxieties which it aroused initially, has stimulated a clearer mutual understanding of dialogue, and has made help available to those wanting to discover how dialogue can be 'the medium of sensitive witness'.

In partnership with the worldwide church

We are told increasingly these days that we live in a global village. As members of the Christian church, and specifically of the Anglican Communion, we are aware of being part of an international community. It is right, therefore, to express appreciation and give due acknowledgement to the way in which the church in other lands has been a stimulus to the work of evangelism in England during this decade.

Several dioceses have made quite specific links between the Decade and their link dioceses in other parts of the world. The Carlisle diocese invited twelve partners from link dioceses to produce a Partners in Mission report for the diocese. This was done in conjunction with an invitation from the bishop to identify its vision for the decade. Both emphasised the need to reach out. As a result of this the Springboard team was invited to visit the diocese on two separate occasions (six months apart) to help stimulate the work of evangelism, with a specific brief to train and equip evangelists. The aim of this process is that global and national resources should be called upon, not to do the Church's work for it, but in order to equip it to do its job more effectively.

In a parallel venture in the Lichfield diocese, the Bishop of Sabah (their link diocese) brought a team of 19 Christians from that diocese for a three week series of events. The diocesan missioner, the Revd Alan Smith, commented about the experience:

> One of the most exciting parts of this cross-cultural mission was the way that our companions from Sabah

were able to speak into our culture. Coming from a totally different background people from the UK were much more open to them than they would be to a mission team from this country. Not only did their visit re-invigorate some of our churches, but a number of people were either renewed in their faith or brought to faith though their visit.

Another way in which the global church has helped forward the work of the Decade has been through the work of missionary societies of various kinds. In the autumn of 1994 the Mothers' Union in the UK arranged for two Training in Evangelism Conferences to be addressed by evangelists from Africa. USPG's Every Nation Under Heaven group, and the CMS World Reach Conference brought people to England from overseas for short visits. All this is in addition to the regular on-going exchange of people and groups in which the mission agencies play a vital role.

Societies such as the Church Mission Society and Crosslinks have given valuable help to churches working with ethnic minority groups, both to understand their culture, and to know how best to enter into dialogue and the communication of the Christian faith. Included in this support has been the provision of resources to enable evangelists from other continents to come for an extended period to work in parishes and dioceses in this country. CMS has also produced two videos. *In the Same Boat* gives an insight into models of evangelism in other parts of the world, whilst *Let My People Grow* gives different examples of evangelism – in inner city Waterloo, multi-faith Luton and among young people. Most societies have a series of structures to enable two-way learning through exchange of personnel and experience to take place. This contribution is commended to the local church as a valuable resource.

At Kanuga, North Carolina, USA

The whole Anglican communion took specific action in promoting the Decade of Evangelism, and in reflecting on its progress, through the calling of a Conference in Kanuga, USA, in September 1995 to report on progress worldwide on the work of evangelism. One hundred and twenty delegates from virtually every province came to share in this conference. Key phrases which emerged at the Conference were 'the gospel for the whole person' and 'integrated, contextual evangelism'. The following extract from the Conference message to the Primates of the Anglican Communion expressing something of the feel and impact it had:

We find it hard to overstate the impact of this Conference on us as delegates, not only because of the breadth of representation and experience, but also because of the challenge to repentance, reconciliation and closer working together that we have received.

Our hearts have been encouraged as we have heard and discussed many stories from all Provinces of the grace of God at work in evangelism and mission. In and through these he is speaking to His Church.

We have been challenged as we have heard of the witness of Christians caught up with peoples in war, poverty and the effects of global inequality. We recognise too the challenge of witness among peoples of other faiths and the struggles of Churches facing decline in Europe, North America and Australasia.

We give thanks to God for many reports of growth in numbers of Christians, for development of Christian spirituality, and, as part of the witness of faith, of Christians taking seriously their engagement with the social needs and the cultures of the societies in which they are set.

From all the reports we have heard we believe there is clear evidence. . . that evangelism is taking a more cental and accepted place in the life of our Churches.

We are particularly concerned both to release the ministry of evangelism throughout the Church and to challenge many aspects of our Church's life that are indifferent to evangelism.

We attach great importance to the role of lay people in evangelism, particularly women. . .We call for attention to be given to evangelism among children and young people.

We recognise that this will involve risks and ventures of faith, but as a Church we are called to walk by faith and trust in a God who so loved the world that he risked His Son to reconcile all things to Himself.

Through the central agencies of the Church of England

It is not possible, within the scope of this report, to do more than highlight some of the ways in the which the central agencies and structures of the Church, including General Synod and the different departments of Church House, have been providing resources for the Decade of Evangelism. Nor is it possible to attempt an assessment of how far there has been a missionary shift in the way that the various Boards and Councils set priorities and do their work. Such a thorough-going review has in fact been done by the Turnbull Report *Working as One Body,* though consideration is currently being given within the Board of Mission to the possibility of developing a contribution to the post-Turnbull debate about the extent of the mission-shift in the central agencies of the church. However, for this report, the following reports and actions need to be identified.

The Howe Commission's report *Heritage and Renewal,* and the Turnbull Report *Working as One Body* are major pieces of work which will shape the work of cathedrals and the central structures of the church for many years to come. Both have emerged out of the mission imperative of the Church; a recognition that existing structures were developed for a very different situation than the one the Church faces today. Both have shaped their response to the changed circumstances around a mission perspective. They witness to the extent to which the missionary shift for which Lambeth 1988 called has taken hold of the thinking of the Church.

The Board of Mission clearly has a particularly crucial role in the work of the Decade of Evangelism. To that end it has established a Decade staff team, helps to mount an annual conference for diocesan missioners, and produces resources to help forward the mission of the church. *All God's Children?* addressed the crucial nature of the Church's engagement with children and young people. *Breaking New Ground*, the report of the House of Bishops, drawn up with the help of the Board, gives guidelines for the new work of church planting. This document is proving a value aid to those working in this area. The occasional paper *Building Missionary Congregations* is a contribution to the making of the missionary shift called for at Lambeth 1988.

On the Way is a report on the practice of Christian initiation. It was produced jointly by the Board of Mission, the Board of Education and the Liturgical Commission. At a time when the whole emphasis on evangelism as a process is gaining ground, it is important that this development is set in the wider context of the thorough initiation of the newcomer to faith. Fine though many modern process approaches to evangelism are, they are unlikely to do the whole work of initiation. The early Church was no doubt right in thinking of this as a three year process. This report calls attention to this deeper work, and to ways

34

in which it is and can be practised. The Church is in need of more resources to help it at just this point.

The Advisory Board of Ministry has engaged with the Decade agenda at a number of points. In its recently revised selection criteria, some further progress has been made towards a more explicitly missionary understanding of the nature of ordained ministry. Mission was also addressed in its earlier report, *Order in Diversity*, though it would also be true to say that much of the criticism of that report was in terms of its limited stress on mission. That criticism is itself evidence of the extent to which missionary thinking is permeating the whole of the church's thinking.

ABM jointly with BOM, hosted an important consultation on the missionary context of training for the ministry in April 1994. Entitled Making Christ Known the consultation drew together over one hundred principals and staff members of theological colleges and courses, together with representatives of BOM and ABM, to consider how mission can be the theme and perspective from which all training for ministry is shaped.

The paper *Ordination and the Church's Ministry* (ABM Ministry Paper No.1), which is an interim evaluation of college and course work expresses clearly the missionary focus of training quoting one document as stating: 'the church exists primarily as a vehicle for God's mission in the world'. There is a growing recognition that mission is the theme around which selection, training and deployment must be constructed and measured.

There is also a growing link between the work of Continuing Ministerial Education officers and diocesan missioners in working out the implications of the BOM report *Building Missionary Congregations*.

A significant part of the work of the Board of Education relates to work among children and young people, to the major work of church schools and to the promotion of adult education. The joint report (with the Board of Mission) of *All God's Children?* has been a major contribution to mission among children and young people. It has yet to be seen whether the Church will grasp the challenge represented by this report to put energies and resources into this area.

Adult education is foundational to the work of mission. Churches which show evidence of engaging in mission are almost invariably those which have harnessed the gifts, abilities and concerns of lay members and released those gifts within and beyond the life of the local church. Education, training and enabling are crucial to that work. In particular the six week course Monday Matters is a valued (and as yet under-used) resource which the Board of Education has made available to the Church in the Decade.

The work of the Board for Social Responsibility 'is mission or it is nothing' (David Skidmore, BSR Secretary). So the Board's contribution to the Decade needs to be seen in terms of enabling the voice of the church(es) to be heard at the national level, shedding the light of the gospel on the whole of human life. It sees the need for gospel values to transform social structures as well as individual lives. To take just one example, the report *Responsibility in Arms Transfer Policy* (GS 1130) showed how Christian values could be brought to bear on the complex ethical dilemmas of the arms trade. Other areas that the Board has addressed in recent years include medical ethics and biotechnology.

The more recent report *Something to Celebrate*, though not without its critics, is intended to serve as a stimulus to the debate taking place in society on the changes which are taking place in patterns of family life. It seeks to identify what can appropriately be affirmed or challenged in those changes. In addition to producing this report, the Board has also helped, alongside the Board of Education and Board of Mission, in the promotion of parenting courses. These courses not only address the concern of parents who are trying to fulfil their responsibilities in the raising of children, but also point to the spiritual basis on which family life should be founded. They are one example of how social action and responsibility and the sharing of faith go together.

The Council for the Care of Churches has sought to engage with the Decade through the production of the report *Mission and Mortar* which addressed the question of how to use the mission potential of the church's buildings. This theme is being further developed at a national conference in 1996, and relates also to the work of the Rural Affairs Committee, and the Tourism Group associated with the Decade and supported by the BOM. This group has been seeking to help 'turn tourists into pilgrims' and to help churches be creative in the literature they make available to the 35 million people who visit churches each year. This figure does not include visitors to cathedrals and major minsters. The *Contact Makers* pack produced by the BOM has material for such churches, which refers enquirers to the Christian Enquiry Agency.

What has been reported here is a small sample of the ways in which the central structures of the Church have taken up the theme of mission and evangelism, have sought to relate their work to that focus in the life of the Church, and have provided valuable resources to that end.

Through the voluntary societies

Very substantial help has been given to the whole Church by the various voluntary agencies in the course of the Decade of Evangelism. The following stand out amongst a much longer list.

The Mothers' Union adopted a three-part strategy for the Decade, each lasting three to four years. That strategy was expressed in these terms:

1. for members to firm up on what they believe and to re-commit themselves to membership of the Church and of the Mothers' Union;

2. for members to gain confidence to go outside the members of the Church, witnessing to the love and forgiveness of God in their daily lives, and sharing their faith with other people in word and action.

3. to draw people, especially young people, into the life and faith of the Church.

To assist in this strategy two courses for groups have been produced. The first, entitled *I Believe and Trust*, sought to give people confidence in their faith. The second, entitled *To Live and Work* seeks to relate personal faith to whole-life issues such as the family and work. These well produced courses have been used by several tens of thousands of Mothers' Union members in the Decade so far.

USPG has developed at the College of the Ascension in Birmingham, a course entitled A New Way of Being Church which is helping people to discover how to implement the Lambeth call for a shift to a missionary orientation in the whole life of the Church. They have also set up a series of root groups, modelled on the base communities of the Church in South America, to give expression to this concern by finding ways of living the faith and being church which relate more naturally to modern culture. Though small numerically, these could be vital pilot projects for a whole new generation of churches in the decades to come.

CPAS has taken as its theme for the first five years that of serving the Decade. It has done so not least in helping to stimulate the 'Seeker-service' approach to worship, and by developing material for group work from the work of various people such as Graham Cray (The Gospel and Tomorrow's Culture), Robert Warren (Launching a Missionary Congregation), Bob Hopkins (Enabling Church Planting) and John Young (Creating Confidence in Evangelism and Live Your Faith). Its evangelism team and youth and children's team, working alongside many parishes, is doing important supportive work for the whole mission of the Church.

The Church Army has not only seconded Capt David Sanderson to work part-time with the Board of Mission's Decade Team. He also edits the Grove Booklets series on evangelism which is proving a valuable resource for many churches.

In response to the Decade, the Church Army has continued its work of training and commissioning evangelists. One area of particular focus is that of church planting where a growing number of evangelists are now working. Other areas include youth work, work with children, with the homeless and with the elderly. They have undertaken a thorough review of all their work and established clear priorities to help them respond more effectively to the challenge of evangelism. They have also determined that all future work funded by them will come within one of their five areas of focus which are: area evangelists, church planting, children and young people, homeless people, older people. In the future they have said that evangelism undertaken by the Church Army will have three important elements, that is to say, words, action and multiplication.

The mission agencies of the Church have also made significant contribution to the work of the Decade, not least in facilitating the 'reverse flow of mission' represented by people from other countries coming to England to assist us in the work of evangelism. A Consultation on the Church of England World Mission Agencies' Contribution to the Decade of Evangelism in England was held in 1992. Its report identifies an extensive list of ways in which this creative 'reverse flow' is taking place.

Whilst recognising, inevitably, that not every agency or society can be named, the above brief list underlines just how vital, and central, the work of voluntary agencies are to the work of evangelism. It is good for the Church to have this opportunity to record its appreciation for their considerable contribution to the Decade of Evangelism.

In preparation for the Decade (1989), and at the mid point in the Decade two major Consultations between Synodical and Voluntary

Bodies in the Church of England were held over a three day period. These were two high-level consultations in which joint planning for the Decade could be developed. The more recent one was developed around the theme Into Missionary Mode.

Through national trends and developments

A further dimension of the work of evangelism can be seen in some significant trends and developments taking place across the whole life of the Church. Four in particular stand out.

Church planting has already been noted as one way in which churches and whole groups of people are seeking to express and share the good news of Jesus Christ. This is an important development in the way the Church of England is expressing its life, and has been recognised and related to the existing structures of the church through the publication of the report *Breaking New Ground*. The rate at which churches are being planted now significantly exceeds the rate at which church buildings are being made redundant.

New worship developments can be seen as an aspect of church planting, but deserves separate comment because of its potential, particularly in communicating the faith to young people. These developments are typically characterised by the development of culturally appropriate expressions of worship. Although this is the most visible aspect of such groups, it is not all there is, or even the most important part. The network of small groups is crucial to the sense of belonging which gives life to such developments. Such initiatives frequently express their life as much in engaging with social needs and issues around them as in 'inculturated worship'. They have much to share with the rest of the Church about effective patterns of initiation and discipleship. There are now dozens of such expressions of the Christian faith, and of Anglican Church life, around the country, drawing on spirituality insights from sources as diverse as Taize and Toronto, and from Celtic, creation and feminist theologies and spiritualities. They could become of growing significance in the years to come, though the tragic circumstances surrounding the Nine O'Clock Service in Sheffield underline the importance of discovering how to establish effective and appropriate structures of accountability. They represent an important, culturally appropriate, expression of the faith among one group with whom the Church is in danger of losing touch.

Process resources relates to courses suitable for those enquiring about the Christian faith. As will be noted later under 'trends in evangelism' this is one of the major developments in recent years in the way that the church is seeking to share its faith. Typically today this happens more in the process of small enquiry groups than in one-off preaching events. For many churches, the development of such groups is the primary way in which they are expressing a commitment to the work of evangelism in this decade.

Spirituality, understood as how we encounter God and how that encounter is sustained is at the heart of the Christian faith. It is also how many in our society today, through the New Age movement, are seeking to make a connection between life and the transcendent. Although the Church would want to criticise much that passes for spirituality in such movements, it also has much to learn from seeing spirituality as the way in to the knowledge of God. It was the contention of medieval mystics that 'evangelism is the sharing of the fruits of our contemplation with others'.

One of the clearest evidences of this trend is the charismatic renewal movement. The fact that one of the aspects of the Church where growth is most often to be located is in churches which are involved in this renewal movement. That movement is essentially a spirituality movement, and as such illustrates the importance of spiritual renewal as lying at the heart of the life of the Church. This movement is well served in the Church of England by Anglican Renewal Ministries (ARM), through their running of conferences, development of resources, and the production of a magazine, *Anglicans for Renewal,* which is widely circulated and appreciated.

Likewise, the Cursillo and Focolare movement, a revival of interest in Celtic and creation spiritualities, the writings and speaking of people such as Gerard Hughes all point to an area of importance for the whole of life, for the life of the Church, and for the work of evangelism. There is evidence that people are coming to faith via this route. The increase in the number of spirituality advisers/officers appointed in many dioceses is to be welcomed.

Missionary congregations is a term first used by the World Council of Churches in their report, *The Church for Others*, published in 1960. That report was subtitled 'the missionary structure of the congregation'. It sought to address the fact that the Church needs to be renewed around its missionary calling, at least as much as around its pastoral work which has hitherto largely shaped how the Church orders its life.

In recent years, and increasingly during the Decade, this theme has been picked up again as various churches and agencies have come to recognise that 'how the Church is the Church' is a major factor in the spread (or hindrance to spreading) of the gospel. It is likely that the second half of the Decade will see a growing interest in this subject. Included under this heading are the following ways in which renewing the life of the local church around its missionary nature is taking place.

This is closely related to the USPG initiative in developing 'root groups'. These have been developed over the past eighteen years. They are small communities of young people committed to incarnating evangelism in the local parish situation for periods of up to a year. These groups are a particularly effective way of both encouraging young people in mission and also giving the opportunity of learning to live in a community as a witness to others.

The Council of Churches for Britain and Ireland (CCBI) has instigated a long-term ecumenical learning process about missionary congregations and has recently appointed a full-time field officer to take forward the work already done in researching what is taking place. It is likely to provide further evidence and resources to help churches consider how their whole life needs to be, and can be, re-orientated around mission.

The Board of Mission's Occasional Paper, *Building Missionary Congregations,* also addresses this issue. This Occasional Paper had to be reprinted within four months of publication. That indicates considerable interest in re-thinking how the church functions today. Developing and applying this work is likely to be a major theme in the second half of the Decade.

QUESTIONS CHURCHES ARE ASKING

What have we been doing so far in the Decade of Evangelism?

What lessons have we learned?

Where in the list of all that has been reported above can we see that we could be more fully engaged in the second half of the Decade?

Where might we look for help to develop the work of evangelism through this church?

3

Assessing the impact
of the Decade so far

The Decade is essentially a commitment of the Church to give particular emphasis to something that must always be a part of its life, namely mission and evangelism. What needs to be assessed is the extent to which there is currently a discernable emphasis on evangelism and renewal of mission-orientation in the whole life of the church. It was this that Lambeth 1988 called for. It is this that needs to be assessed.

The assessment which follows looks in turn at the signs of a new mission perspective and the signs of sustainable growth in the work of evangelism. It also considers the statistical evidence and attempts to identify what has not yet been achieved in the Decade.

Signs of a new mission perspective

There is much to encourage the Church in what has been reported in the previous section. What is recounted there is only a small sample of what is being done. Clearly much is happening, many new initiatives have been taken and, in a great number of different areas of the Church's life, there is clear evidence that the Church is grappling with mission in creative ways. Some of the encouraging signs are as follows:

The Decade has put evangelism and mission on the Church's agenda. One woman deacon said 'The Decade of Evangelism has made a tremendous difference to our church. It has put evangelism onto the agenda'. She then added: 'We still can't do it; but it is on the agenda.' In fact the church she serves is a typical urban 'middle of the road' parish that has taken great strides in engaging with the practice of evangelism in recent years. However, in churches where evangelism has reached only as far as the agenda, that step in itself marks considerable progress. More needs to happen, but talking about it can be the first step towards action.

The Decade has stimulated many local and diocesan initiatives. Practically every diocese has sought to engage with the focus of the

Decade in some way. The Decade has given rise to a vast range of different initiatives.

The Decade has seen a great increase in the level of attendance at training events. The support and active encouragement by diocesan bishops is almost invariably connected to this growth in attendance. It indicates a readiness by many to learn new skills in spreading of the faith.

The Decade has significantly shaped the way that the church is handling it resources. From the Turnbull Report, *Working as One Body*, at the centre, to the various re-structuring schemes in most dioceses, it is clear that 're-structuring for mission' is the common agenda.

The Decade has affected the perspective within General Synod debates. In some ways this can be seen most clearly when Synod is responding to reports presented to it. The debates about reports such as *Mission in Mortar*, and *Order in Diversity*, as well as in challenging the dropping of the grant to the Christian Enquiry Agency, demonstrate that the question 'how, and how well, does this help to forward the Church's mission' is a primary yardstick by which General Synod now tests such reports. It was not always so.

Signs of sustainable growth in the work of evangelism

Although it is not possible to separate out the impact of the Decade from other factors (whether having a positive or a negative effect), there are a number of indications which represent healthy signs within the life of the Church.

First, is the growth in process or enquirer groups. Although there are no independent figures available, the reports from a number of agencies indicate that there is a strong growth in the development of enquirer groups. The Mothers' Union reports that 68,000 people have been through the I Believe and Trust Course. The Alpha Course claims that 100,000 people will go through the Alpha course in 1995; with the potential for double that number in 1996. Not all, but most, of those are in Anglican churches. Each month, at present, approximately two hundred churches register as starting their first Alpha course. If the actual figure is only half that number it still represents a major development. Moreover, it is important to remember that although Alpha is the 'process course' which has had the most publicity, it is only one of a wide range of such courses (see under Trends in Evangelism for details of other courses). Many other similar courses report an increasing take-up and implementation of their materials.

Second is the increase in church planting in recent years. This is now currently running at the rate of about one new congregation per week being established nationally. It is interesting to note that in the first three years of the Decade 102 'church plants' were begun. During the same period 84 church buildings were made redundant. This means the Church of England is currently increasing the number of its churches, whilst continuing to reduce the number of its buildings.

Third is the growth of alternative, or new, expressions of worship and church life. Whilst there is much that the Church has yet to learn about how best to handle and integrate these into the existing patterns of church life, such expressions, usually developed among young people or young adults, are of significance well beyond the actual numbers of people involved. The youthful energy and commitment to the Christian faith and its expression in a vibrant Anglican form represented by these groups is suggestive of new life coursing through Anglican veins.

Fourth is the increasing attendance at training days and courses. This has been noted above. Several dioceses have had two thousand people attending single training events. More typical is the small course and group which are attracting higher attendances. The church seems ready to learn.

It is important to note the word 'sustainable' in the heading of this section. The Decade, perhaps many feared, would be a sudden, and unsustainable, burst of evangelistic activity at the end of which the church would collapse exhausted. Although such an approach might have grabbed the headlines, it would not have been good news for the church or the gospel. In fact this has not happened. Rather, a steady turning of attention and energy to evangelism as central to the whole life of the Church is taking place. This bodes well for the work of evangelism beyond the end of the Decade.

Signs of church growth?

The Decade of Evangelism is a commitment to tell those beyond the Church the good news of Jesus Christ. As such, part of the goal is to see an increase in the number of people participating in the life of the Church. However, that is not the only goal or exclusive measure of mission. The prophets of old, the parable of the sower, and the life of Christ all remind us that good news is not always treated as such and acted upon, and yet needs to be made known.

The Decade is essentially intended to encourage the Church to be outward looking and to be strengthened in its calling to 'make Christ known', whatever the response. Nonetheless, the growth of the church is a worthy goal, even if it is not the primary focus of the Decade.

It is right, therefore, to look for any statistical evidence of Church growth resulting from the Decade of Evangelism. Such statistics as are available are produced by the Central Board of Finance (see *Church Statistics, 1995*). In considering these figures the following points need to be borne in mind.

The context in which the Decade was launched is one of long-term decline in membership of all the main-stream Churches, including the Church of England. That decline has been happening for over a hundred years. It has affected not only the Church of England but also the Free Churches and (more recently) the Roman Catholic church. This decline is evident across the whole of Europe; and indeed affects other institutions too, such as political parties, social organisations, and trade unions, all of which are experiencing decline in paid-up membership. Some encouragement may be taken from the fact that since 1968 as the graph shows, the decline has slowed down, though it has not yet been arrested.

This decline has continued in the first four years of the Decade. So, for example, usual Sunday attendance has dropped from 1.14m in 1990 to 1.09m in 1994, and confirmations have dropped from sixty thousand in 1990 to forty eight thousand in 1994.

However, it is important to bear in mind the following points.

The decline in church attendance is not matched by a decline in religious awareness. Whilst attendance figures have declined for a long period, measures of religious perception, experience and practice, indicate a continuing religious background in society today. This has been highlighted by Grace Davie in *Religion in Britain since 1945*, in which she coins the phrase 'believing without belonging' as character- istic of contemporary society, commenting: 'Why relatively high levels of belief and low levels of practice should be considered normal is far from clear'. (Grace Davie, *Religion in Britain,* p.5) A recent MORI poll showed that while only about 10% of the population are active church goers, 88% wanted to call themselves Christian. Similar percentages are regularly registered when people are asked if they believe in God and if they pray. Christian values and beliefs are still widely held by a population in Britain which goes to church only occasionally.

The overall picture obscures some important positive signs.
Included in these signs are the following:

1. The rate of decline has slowed down since the late 1980s. This is shown in the graph below. It may well be due to the fact that a third of churches have begun to identify factors which encourage growth.

Total USA from 1968 to 1993

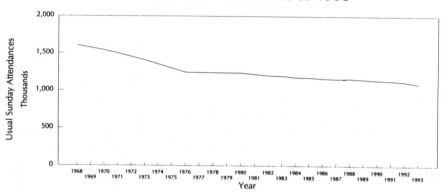

usual Sunday attendance from 1968 to 1993

2. Major variations are obscured by taking an overall view. Some churches, and types of churches, are growing, whilst others are experiencing continued decline. There are also wide regional variations, for example from 13 Anglican worshippers per 1000 of population in Birmingham to 42 per 1000 in Hereford (*Church Statistics,* Table 38). Work needs to be done to establish the causes of this, and the lessons from such variations.

3. Major demographic changes mask significant mission engagement. We live in a multi-faith society. This inevitably changes the role and impact of the church. For example, one church in a Northern industrial town has 50 worshippers. However, it is in a parish where there are only 100 non-muslim people living in the area, and where the church has contributed significantly to the healing of racial tensions in the area. The statistics do not reflect the value of the work of that church; rather, they mask important work and witness.

4. Changing patterns of regular church going are not reflected in these figures. There is widespread anecdotal evidence to suggest that 'regular worshipper' now means 'two or three times a month' rather than the former 'once a Sunday'. This is no doubt related to the fact

that families are living further away from each other, both because of social mobility, and because of the break up of families. There is also probably some impact from the changes in Sunday trading and leisure activities. This change in patterns of church attendance is not reflected in the figures, which may actually be evidence that slightly more people are going to church, but less often. Again work needs to be done to establish if this is the case.

5. The level of giving has been increasing – above the rate of inflation. Weekly average covenanted giving per subscriber was £4.52 in 1993 (the last year for which accurate figures are available). This has risen in real terms from an average of £3.77 in 1990 (a 20% increase in just three years). The total ordinary income of PCCs has risen in real terms from £265m in 1990 to £287m in 1993. These two sets of figures suggest a Church with a strong sense of commitment. The Central Board of Finance's Stewardship Committee have agreed that there is anecdotal evidence supported by some statistical information that giving in some UPA parishes is proportionately higher than in other areas (*Staying in the City,* paragraph 4.63). The Church would do well to explore this further and see what could be learned from this pattern.

6. Specific areas do reflect growth. See the comments under the section above (signs of sustainable growth) about the increase in enquirer groups, church planting, alternative worship and training.

In short, whilst there are some encouraging signs, there is much in the situation of the Church in England (and not just the Church of England) which presents a challenge to the Church. Our faith requires that we ask hard questions about how the Church is handling its life, and how it can be more effective in communicating its faith.

The Church would be well served by the establishing of a group of people, or piece of work, to look behind the global figures, available from the Central Board of Finance, with a view to identifying the trends that are life-giving and the trends of decline which need to be addressed. All that this report can to do is to urge the church to invest some resources in learning all it can from a complex situation.

The competing agendas?

The work of mission and evangelism has had to battle hard for priority in the first half of the Decade in view of the competing agendas raised by the decision to ordain women and by the major impact of the losses of the Church Commissioners. These massive agendas have consumed vast amounts of time and emotion. They could have completely stalled the whole work of the Decade. It is a tribute to the church that that has not happened, as the reporting section above makes abundantly clear.

In fact, in many places, these very issues have become not competing and distracting agendas, but rather significant expressions of the implication and outworking of the gospel, as explained in the section above entitled by women shows on pages 26-8.

It is to be hoped that as the Church enters the second half of the Decade, there will be a renewal of commitment to give the work of evangelism the priority it deserves. If that can be done, and major alternative agendas held in check, the second half of the Decade could well built very positively upon the first half.

The multiple agenda

If the Decade cannot be required to bear the weight of reversing the trend of decline in church attendance, then what can? The state and impact of the Church, in the course of its history, seems to be related to three factors which interact on each other. They are as follows:

First, the Divine will. It is not particularly within the world view of our present society to allow for the purposes of God. However, the Church which has been taught to pray 'your kingdom come' knows that there are times and seasons when the message is heard, and times when it meets with resistance. This is why prayer is always a first order priority for the Church – prayer for the coming of God's kingdom, prayer for the needs of his world, and prayer for discernment about our part in his purposes.

Second, the state of the Church. It can be an aid or an obstacle to the communication of the gospel. A number of voices are calling the Church at present, in the midst of profound changes taking place in society, to discover 'new ways of being church'. There is a gospel imperative in this. However, it is important that the Church does not come to believe that what it does will, in and of itself, bring in the Kingdom of God.

Third, the state of the surrounding community. There are times when communities seem open to the Christian message and times when they are – relatively speaking – closed. Faithfulness requires that the gospel is spoken into both situations. However, that faithfulness cannot be measured in terms of numerical success.

The unfinished agenda

Whilst there is much to affirm, and indeed celebrate, about what has been done in the first half of the Decade, it is also necessary – in a document such as this – to identify what has not yet been achieved. The following points stand out. They are not intended to be read as criticisms of what has been done so far, but rather as pointers to what has yet to be accomplished.

First, whilst getting evangelism onto the agenda of the Church, the Decade has not yet got the good news onto the lips of church members in any great measure. That must be a priority for the second half of the Decade. Hence the prominence of 'naming the Name' in the shaping section with which this report ends.

Second, more has been done by way of evangelistic endeavours than has been done in changing the inner culture of many churches. Whilst not losing the readiness to tell good news, it is vital that the Church learns in deeper measure to live it – in culturally appropriate ways – if believing and belonging are to become one in any significant measure.

Third, whilst many churches have developed specific evangelism initiatives, there are still many churches that have yet to engage seriously with the implications of the Decade. It may well be that archdeacons' visitations are one way of uncovering such situations and then of finding ways of enabling those churches to join with the rest.

Fourth, though 'restructuring for mission' is virtually always now identified as the goal of restructuring, retrenchment is sometimes what is actually being managed. Perhaps the key test of this distinction is the identification as to where resources are being released to forward mission. If no resources are being put into development then only retrenchment is happening.

These are some of the issues that need to be addressed in the second half of the Decade. Specific proposals about how they should be addressed are contained in the section on developing the second half of the Decade.

QUESTIONS CHURCHES ARE ASKING

How do we assess the impact of the Decade of Evangelism on our church?

What are the implications of that assessment for the future?

4

Assessing the 1994 national initiatives

Considerable publicity was given in 1994 to a series of national initiatives in evangelism. The reason for there being several within a matter of a few months should be explained. The Group for Evangelisation of the Council of Churches for Britain and Ireland has sought, in response to many requests, to attempt both to co-ordinate, channel and, where necessary, contain, the enthusiasm of those inclined to attempt high profile (and high energy consuming) initiatives. To this end they agreed, early in the Decade, to try to limit national initiatives to 1994, 1997 and the year 2000. It was for this reason that the bi-annual ecumenical Lent course was developed as the national initiative for 1994. Independently of GFE a group of people came up with the On Fire! plans. They were quick to seek ecumenical and denominational support and were willing to be guided by others about their plans. They were sufficiently different (and distant in timing) from Have Another Look, for a decision to be made to agree to support the project. Then, quite fortuitously – and obviously without any reference to other denominations or ecumenical groups (other than invitations to take part) – two other national initiatives were also mounted. These two initiatives were the Pentecostal Churches' JIM campaign, and the Reinhard Bonke distribution of the *Minus to Plus* booklet to every household in the United Kingdom. Both were planned to take place in the same four month period which spanned the other two initiatives. It seems to have been a matter of 'the best laid plans of mice and men. . .' only compounding the problem.

However, all four events went ahead, often to the confusion of church members who, after a few years of no national initiatives, were suddenly faced with four in as many months.

Have Another Look. This was a Lent course designed to be run with enquirers into the faith. It was developed by the Council of Churches for Britain and Ireland, and was part of a pattern of developing such ecumenical material in alternate years in Lent. It was intended that new groups should be formed for this purpose, though often existing home groups were used. It was one of the most widely used Lent course ever to take place, with an estimated attendance of between 150,000 to 200,000 people involved.

The groups rarely attracted a significant number of enquirers. It should be pointed out that the very concept of a Lent course is something that, whilst meaning something to church members, is not likely to connect immediately with non-church members. Many would have no idea what 'Lent' means. Many would find a meeting in a home a threatening prospect.

What the groups do seem to have achieved is further ecumenical strengthening, and the development of church members' confidence to speak about their faith. Some groups were able to introduce new people to the faith and the worshipping life of the local church.

JIM Campaign. This advertising-led campaign to 'ask JIM' (where 'JIM' means 'Jesus in me') was developed by the Pentecostal Churches of Great Britain. It was hampered by the lack of access to television advertising, and by being a rushed operation. The aim was to see 250,000 people come to faith.

In practice the response of churches was patchy. Where a number of churches in a locality worked together there was some significant impact, whilst in other areas the idea never took off. As with Have Another Look, considerable co-operation among churches was achieved. Since Pentecostal churches have tended to be separate from other churches, this was a significant gain. The project would almost certainly have benefitted greatly from taking an extra year to plan and implement.

Minus to Plus. This was a mailing intended to reach every home, developed by the Christ for All Nations organisations run by Reinhard Bonke. It gained the most publicity though was of very limited effectiveness. Distribution of the booklet (not, contrary to popular understanding, by the Post Office) was really quite poor. Some postal areas, where churches had trained scores of counsellors, were simply missed out altogether. The organisers claimed a 75% success in mailing every home, but few independent observers would put it as high as 50%. The organisers had been led to expect a 20% response, despite the fact that – before the event – people with experience of such free distribution operations were saying that the norm was 0.5%. It was the latter figure which was borne out by the response. A total of 20,000 response forms were returned. After allowing for school children filling in the form for 'friends' in order to embarrass them, for compulsive form fillers, and for forms filled by church members, the impact was very small, especially considering the £5m cost.

On Fire! Developed originally by Steve Chalke (a Baptist minister) of Oasis Trust, this became an ecumenical project. The aim was to encourage local events in celebration of Pentecost to which fringe members of the church could be invited. One of its unfortunate problems was that the day designated was one of the wettest days nationally in the whole year. However, the project was one of the most useful of the four events, though it largely drew church members – and only the courageous and fool-hardy at that, in view of the weather. Again, it would certainly have benefitted from having at least one further year to plan and publicise. One of the strengths of this event was the process it gave for future national initiatives. The idea was conceived and communicated nationally, but it allowed for a great deal of creative interpretation at the local level. Certainly, imposed initiatives and structures are likely to fare poorly in today's climate. A creative idea that can be interpreted and implemented locally seems to be a model that can be repeated. It is certainly suggestive as to how the millennium celebrations might be handled.

The overall impression of these four events is that they were limited in their effectiveness. Enormous amounts of effort by many church members, and vast sums of money (especially in the case of *Minus to Plus*) were expended with limited impact. One cannot but contrast them with the impact in the same year of the various nurture courses identified above which cost very little, probably brought more people to faith that these four initiatives together, and will be doing the same (and may well be a growing practice for several years to come yet) for each of the remaining years of the decade.

Moreover it has to be acknowledged that these sort of major initiatives, whilst having a limited impact, can often have a profound impact on the use of limited resources. Whilst there is a place for major and national initiatives, the Church needs to protect itself from their proliferation. However, it may be right to see that some temperaments within the Church are more attracted to the major campaign/initiative approach and that a place should be built into the Church's programme for those with such motivation. These initiatives, however, present something of a cautionary tale for those who venture into these fields in the future.

5

Identifying trends in society

Society is always changing. Yet there are times when those changes become profound and epoch making. It is rather like the continental plates in earthquake areas. The plates are always on the move, but sometimes a move creates a cataclysmic event on the surface which no one can miss. Among such times of major upheaval, in the present millennium, is the age of the Reformation and Renaissance at the beginning of the sixteenth century, and the time of Revolution at the end of the eighteenth century when France and America both experienced Revolution, and England experienced the spiritual awakening under the Wesleys. Today we are in another such period of major upheaval. As the trappist monk, Thomas Merton, put it:

> We are living in the greatest revolution in history, a huge, spontaneous upheaval of the entire human race. . .This is not something we have chosen or are free to avoid.

The implications of this for the Church, for all institutions and organisations, and indeed for all people, is vast. Some of the finest minds have sought to discern where it is all leading, and what are the wellsprings of this fundamental change. Necessarily, the task of this analysis is more limited. Its specific purpose is to identify some of the ways in which the massive change affecting all of society impinges on the work of evangelism and mission.

The aim here, therefore, is simply to identify some of the factors affecting the culture in which we live, with a view to seeing how they might affect the way we seek to express the faith. It is tempting to label these 'positive' and 'negative' factors. Yet the 'positive factors' can lead people in the wrong direction (e.g. the hunger for spirituality or belonging can make the sects look very attractive to some people); and the 'negative factors' (such as the breakdown in community or the consumer culture) can bring people up short to recognise that change is needed.

What the Church can do is to pray for the discernment to know how far we should welcome each trend, how far we should adjust to it, or how far this is a trend we need to confront. This was a point made powerfully by Bishop David Gitari at the Lambeth Conference of 1988 (see Tom and Barbara Butler's, *Just Mission,* pages 73-74). The task in this section is simply to identify the issues about which the Church needs to seek discernment.

Bewildering change

Alvin Tofler, in his book *Future Shock,* was one of the first people to alert us to the, literally 'shocking', impact not only of the changes taking place in society, but the sheer rate of change. It may well be that our whole culture is in shock. Certainly shock waves have been emanating from a great range of different epicentres.

Vast political upheavals have taken place in recent years. We have witnessed the collapse of communism at the end of the eighties. We have seen the tragic 'implosion' of whole nations under the impact of deep internal tensions. The former state of Yugoslavia, and Rwanda, being two of the most horrific. Northern Ireland has some of the characteristics of the same internal tensions, though the guns have been mercifully quiet for over a year now. We have witnessed the wonderful transformation of South Africa from apartheid to 'a rainbow people', no doubt with vast problems remaining, yet essentially a good news story of hope for others. Such is the scale of change within our own culture that some have questioned the stability of the West – the side that was meant to have 'won' the Cold War.

Economic changes, with job insecurity rapidly becoming a way of life for many, are continually being fuelled by the technological and information revolutions. Great social upheaval can be seen in the increasing break up of the family, and in the rapid disappearance of most social norms. For example, the number of couples cohabiting before marriage has risen from 6% twenty years ago to 60% today. The result of all this change is that fixed reference marks in life have lost their stabilising effect. For example, you can no longer trust that work, or the family, will be there when you need them.

One of the major responses to so much change at so many levels is that of retreat. That retreat takes a number of forms. For some it is retreat out of living, into watching others live out make-believe lives in television soap operas. Retreat often takes people into the privatised world of the individual, family, or part-family. For others retreat is into any of a vast range of addictions – 'to medicate intolerable reality'. For the Church the danger of such retreat lies in the temptations to fundamentalism and traditionalism – rather than in the re-working of the tradition and the fundamentals in a new setting. Rather, as Terry Waite has put it:

> Our fragmented society needs a whole series of 'reflective pools', places where the very deepest issues of life and death may be explored and understood away from the cut and thrust of the market place.
> *Taken on Trust.*

The Church needs to find out how it can avoid becoming a bolt-hole from life, but rather a watering hole on the pilgrimage of life and faith.

Churches are responding by

* *embracing a thoughtful recognition that change is good*

* *going back to scripture and the Church's tradition to find resources for this new situation*

* *establishing groups where these changes can be faced and reflected upon*

* *developing an ostrich mentality and spirituality (not recommended!).*

Rejection of authority

A major change has taken place in our society in relation to our attitude to authority. The roots of this change can probably be traced back to the questioning approach of the scientific thinking which emerged at the time of the Renaissance. A child of that questioning is the development of democracy, growing out of a conviction that the led should have some say in who the leaders are. It has further developed into a view of the equality of all and the right of everyone to have a say in decisions.

Alongside this is the rejection of all external-to-the-self authority, in terms either of imposed moral codes, or of someone's 'right' to tell me what to think or do. In view of the major emphasis in the Church on authority (whether Catholic Pope, Protestant Bible, or Anglican mix of scripture and tradition). This has a profound effect on how the Church communicates its message. It would seem that it can no longer start by saying 'the Church says. . .' or 'the Bible says. . .' and expect that to carry authority.

Related to this is the post-modern view that 'there are no meta-narratives now'. That near-jargon statement is saying that there is a widespread rejection of any overarching world view which attempts to explain everything. Whilst it needs to be pointed out that the view that 'there are no meta-narratives now' is itself a 'meta-narrative', there clearly is a major new situation for the Church to face here.

It would seem that the only readily accepted authority is the Self, but that is necessarily of limited value since one person's experience of truth is recognised as just that – authentic for them, but not necessarily for anyone else. Hence the phrase in some popular psychology about 'experiencing your reality' as something unique to that individual.

Churches are responding by

* *reworking leadership patterns around enabling, empowering and collaborative principles*

* *affirming the value of visionary leadership in the context of shared responsibility*

* *developing permission-giving attitudes and structures*

* *facing conflict, rather than suppressing it.*

Cynicism

The very nature of the scientific/technological culture in which we live is a questioning one. 'How does it work?' 'How can we make it work?' 'Prove it!' are the terms in which scientific enquiry is developed. Valid though it is for such enquiry it is an inappropriate way of proceeding in other aspects of life. Can we prove someone loves us, or that a sunset, or piece of poetry, is beautiful? Does it add anything to the love or the beauty if we can? Certainly such an attitude to life makes faith seem foolish, blind, or a foreign language.

Added to this is the impact of often intrusive media which has added to a cynicism about the motives of any with power or wealth or authority. This is evidenced in a deep seated lack of trust of politicians on the one hand, and most institutions on the other. Faith, and thinking or speaking with faith about the motives of others, appears to be counter-culture.

Churches are responding by

* *deliberately practising affirmation of people and an attitude of thanksgiving towards life*

* *rediscovering a spirituality which affirms both human frailty and human value.*

Consumer culture

Though much of the world is breaking apart into small 'tribal' grouping (witness the break up of the communist countries and the former state of Yugoslavia) there is also a 'Western veneer' which seems to cover the face of the globe – or an ever increasing amount of it.

Consumer culture is essentially a flight from the vulnerability of being human, into the amassing of possession. This is often fed by a false sense that we can make ourselves secure through owning possessions. Only then, we need massive security/defence systems to protect what we have gained. And all the time we are found to be worshipping the creature rather than the creator.

It has been argued by some that the sense of the transcendent, and of the spiritual dimension of life, has been displaced into material possessions. Amassing them has become for many the all-consuming passion of life. Certainly the lottery and the plethora of scratch cards that now abound are giving people (a false) hope of untold riches just around the corner. In reality, they are likely to have the effect of making the poor poorer still.

Churches are responding by

* *an emphasis on the joy of giving and the ability to celebrate*

* *re-establishing co-operatives, thrift shops, OAP meals, soup kitchens, etc*

* *offering a variety in worship, aware of the wide variation in personality/ spirituality types*

* *highlighting Third World needs and events like One World Week and Christian Aid Week.*

Individualism

Arguably since the Reformation and Renaissance in the early 1500s, the shift in religious perception has been away from thinking of creation and of an overarching divine plan for human history and towards the 'assured findings of modern science' with a focus on the self as the 'thinking subject'. That has worked away over several centuries to produce a highly individualistic culture. Indeed, the early meaning of 'individual' meant that we are all one – we are 'indivisible' – whereas today it means the opposite. Particularly since the 'sexual revolution of the sixties', this has led to a great emphasis on the self as the centre of all that is. This is part of the reason for the attractiveness of New Age spiritualities, with the slogan 'I am my own divinity'.

The Church has sometimes been captive to this particular spirit of the age, and has tended to interpret salvation and the gospel in an increasingly individualistic, privatised, and spiritualised way. The conversion written into the very structure of the Lord's Prayer, in which we focus on God first, make ourselves available to his purposes in the world next, and only then bring our needs to him, has been quietly by-passed.

All too easily we have compounded that compromise by preaching against 'individualism' at just the wrong point. Becoming truly ourselves is at the heart of the gospel. Jesus, in his dealings with a great range of people, from Zacchaeus to the woman at the well, and from the rich young ruler to blind Bartimaeus or the woman caught in adultery, called people into the fullness of their humanity. That sort of wholeness and celebration of the worth and uniqueness of the individual is to be affirmed. When that happens we can point to the fact that we become fully human by living in the two great commandments – by turning outwards to love God and others. In belonging, not isolation, we find ourselves.

There are many destructive spin-offs to this development of individualism. It is obviously destructive of community. Moreover, too easily, it results in monochrome groups who reinforce each others identity and then demonise other groups – particularly racially differentiated groups. It also has a corrosive effect on community and provokes people to put up barriers to 'belonging' or any significant involvement with others.

Churches are responding by

* *identifying the unique gifts of each member of the church and affirming them*

* *helping to buy, or run, village post offices in danger of being closed*

* *developing cell-groups as 'little communities' where natural community has broken down.*

Fragmentation

No doubt related to the all-pervading individualism in society today, there is a growing fragmentation of life. This is evidenced in the break up of many families through divorce. It is seen also in the breakdown of local, natural, community, and in the reversion to ethnic groupings evident in such tragic ways in the former state of Yugoslavia and in Rwanda.

The sheer mobility of life further fragments community, as people find their lives broken up into various more or less self-contained worlds of home, leisure, work and local neighbourhood. The growing incidence of 'home alone' cases, and of people being discovered dead in their homes after several days or even weeks of nobody noticing, all point to this shattering of natural human ties of community.

Churches are responding by

* *mounting events which help local communities to find unity (e.g. VE, VJ events)*

* *welcoming of links – especially personal visits – with overseas dioceses and churches*

* *working collaboratively, and ecumenically*

* *emphasising a spirituality which focuses on wholeness, community and love*

* *welcoming diversity as a part of life and of worship.*

Whilst the trends already identified, are – broadly speaking – factors that make it more difficult to speak the Christian message into today's society, there are other factors that lend themselves to such communication. These, potentially (but by no means necessarily) more helpful trends, are identified below.

The search for justice

From the controversial growth of top executive pay on the one hand to the explosion of cardboard cities in our own country on the other, there is clear evidence of the development of an 'underclass' and of a growing gulf between rich and poor. This is of concern to all both because it is a classic cause of the breakdown of societies when inequalities reach overwhelming levels, and because of the sheer injustice involved.

This divide is both in our own nation and between nations. The interest in ethical investments is also evidence of a moral concern in a culture we seem to be shaped entirely by selfish and materialistic interests.

Churches are responding by

* supporting work like Traidcraft, sometimes opening shops which sell such goods

* speaking of, and encouraging, ethical investments

* continued support of Church Urban Fund, and CUF projects.

* working alongside other groups working for justice

* getting involved in Broad Based Organising (via Citizen Organising Foundation).

Care of the environment

The dangers to the environment, from acid rain to the hole in the ozone layer, and from the destruction of rain forests to the extinction of many species of plants and animals, are well documented – even though we all too easily turn a blind eye to our part in this destruction. However, this is arguably the greatest threat to humanity's continued existence on this planet since the ending of the Cold War.

Certainly, both the trends just noted (the gulf between rich and poor, and the environment) are major concerns for the young today. A Church that fails to address and to have integrity about its own handling of these issues is unlikely to connect with youth culture today.

Churches are responding by

* establishing groups which discuss and act on green issues

* sensitive management of churchyards.

Searching for roots

One response to bewildering change is to search for roots, whether in the family tree, the celebration of the solstice at Stonehenge, or in pilgrimages to Holy Island. This may well be one of the factors that prompts 35 million people every year to visit parish churches (that figure excludes the cathedrals and major minsters). Certainly the Christian heritage is a major root of Western civilisation.

Churches are responding by

* *developing ways of harnessing an interest in church buildings to the exploration of faith*
* *creating literature than can help turn tourists into pilgrims*
* *opening and manning churches more often*
* *engaging with, and promoting, Celtic spirituality.*

A hunger for belonging

No doubt as a reaction to the isolation that results from an unhealthy and isolated individualism, there are signs that people are looking for community. Certainly this is what the sects and cults are providing, though all too often in a controlling and destructive way. It is the focus of many magazine articles, usually offering techniques of sexual intimacy as the answer to the loneliness endemic in human existence.

Churches are responding by

* *emphasising the communal, rather than institutional, nature of the Church wherever possible*
* *establishing welcome teams and welcome groups which help people belong from the start.*

A search for identity

The search for meaning in life and for identity is a universal quest. However, the individualism and fragmentation of society have eroded the sense of belonging in which we normally find much of our identity. Moreover, the erosion of moral norms has further hampered the healthy development of people's sense of meaning and purpose in life. If that purpose is reduced to 'doing your own thing' and if you do not know who you are, it can create great anxiety and insecurity. It is at that point that people become vulnerable to sects and to any simple all-consuming focus in life.

Churches are responding by

* *affirming the worth, value and contributions of every member*
* *slowing down the pace of church life and focusing on being more than doing.*

A desert of hope

Where the twentieth century opened with such a strong sense of progress and confidence, it is ending on a sober note of recognition of how little progress we have made, how badly we have damaged the environment, and how little we know about any realistic way forward. There is a major 'famine of hope' in the West, according to Mother Teresa.

The cynicism noted earlier, together with the sheer weight of problems created by, rather than solved by, our technological society, and the loss of moral certainties associated with the rejection of any authority external to the Self, have left a desert of hope. Moreover, the growing gulf between rich and poor has put many people in a situation which seems without hope. Much of the boredom and criminal activity of some young people stems from this same 'hopelessness' about life and about gaining access to the materialistic culture by which their parents have lived.

Churches are responding by

* *focusing on the need for hope in the world in Sunday intercessions*

* *recognising and supporting, not least in Sunday worship, of people in positions of influence*

* *approaching the present crises in the church by renewing hope in God.*

The spiritual dimension

There are some pointers which would indicate that the failure of materialism to meet the deepest hungers in the human heart are beginning to be recognised. 'There must be more to life than an upturn in the economy' is how some are expressing this concern.

This search is also related to a desire, after all the analysis of our technological culture, to 'put life back together again'. The development of New Age thinking and practices is evidence of this hunger for connection with one another, with creation, and with the transcendent dimension in life.

There are many false trails here, with spiritualities which turn into controlling cults, with others that require a total rejection of rational thought, and with yet others that are narcissistic in nature and cut themselves off from the sufferings of this world.

Churches are responding by

* *developing lay training courses, and spirituality courses*

* *running prayer schools*

* *promotion of retreats and quiet days.*

QUESTIONS CHURCHES ARE ASKING

How far does the life, and spirituality, practised by this church represent the living of Christian answers to the concerns of our culture as identified in the above section?

How can the desire of some, to hide from the issues of the complex and changing world in which we live, be addressed?

How could our church set about relating its life more evidently to these concerns in our world today?

4

Identifying enriching trends
in evangelism

The aim of this section is to identify the new directions which are emerging in the practice of evangelism. This is important for several reasons. It alerts us to the changes taking place. It explodes the myth that evangelism is about 'button-holing people on the street'. It gives a check-list against which local churches can assess the appropriate patterns of evangelism which are currently assumed and/or practised. It gives suggestions about how action in evangelism can be enriched by being connected to what the wider Church is discovering.

One of the striking things that has been happening in the first half of the Decade, and in the years immediately prior to its start, has been a significant shift in the way that evangelism is being done. The striking thing about these trends is that no one person or organisation is implementing, imposing, or orchestrating such changes. Rather they seem to be the spontaneous and often instinctive reaction of local churches, and individuals, in the way that they attempt to set about the work of evangelism. Change, and the ability to adapt to new circumstances, are a sign of life. These trends suggest an underlying health in the Body of Christ, which shows a clear ability to adjust to a rapidly changing situation. No doubt, in the light of the previous section about changes in society, these shifts in evangelism reflect the shifts taking place in society today. It is hoped that the following list of trends will help the church to understand what is going on in the area of evangelism, and why some things are working and others are not.

In developing this list careful consideration was given as to whether each point should be set in the formula 'from. . .to. . .', or 'adding. . . to. . .'. An explanation as to why the sharper form has been adopted is in place. Yes, the first word in each trend represents an aspect of evangelism that needs to be retained; it is not being argued that 'events', 'doctrine' or 'speaking', etc., should be abandoned. However, simply suggesting that, for example we add 'spirituality' to 'doctrine' (as in the third trend on page 69) fails to do justice to two things.

It does not highlight sufficiently the different starting point of contemporary evangelism on the one hand; nor does it make clear enough the need to re-work how we communicate doctrine in the light of this shift to spirituality. Whilst the first element in each trend needs to be retained, it is also vital that it is re-worked. Significant unlearning of outmoded and inappropriate ways of doing evangelism that needs to take place. This is particularly so with models of evangelism which are transatlantic in origin. Changing the way that some forms of evangelism are done may well have to include challenging those methods and styles.

Evangelism that flourishes into the third millennium, in other words, will include both aspects of each trend (hence the 'enriched' qualification in the heading of this section), but it will also require major review, renewal with unlearning of outmoded ways of doing evangelism. It is for these reasons that the 'from. . .to. . .' formula has been chosen. However, let it be said again, this is expressing the need for the renewal, not abandoning, of the first element.

At the end of each section some suggestions are made about the questions which the local church could usefully ask itself, together with some suggestions about possible resources that could help in this particular area. It is hoped that many congregations and PCCs will study this section and discern what action they might take in the light of it.

From event to process

Evangelism today is typically carried out in groups, over a series of meetings, in which enquirers can ask questions and engage with Christians at the personal level. This is evidenced in the development already noted of nurture groups as a major expression of the Decade. Such an approach fits better with a culture in which the background information of the faith can no longer be assumed, in which people make up their own minds rather than look to some external authority to tell them what to think or do, and in which the process of experience-reflection-action forms the basis of learning.

Put differently, it can be said that the 'evangelistic appeal' has changed from 'I want you to get up out of your seat and come forward now. . .', to 'we invite you to join a group that will be exploring the Christian faith over the coming weeks at. . .'.

Behind this shift in practice lies a shift in perception, namely that faith is a journey and something that takes time. Coming to faith itself, not just the work of evangelism, is now seen as a process. John Finney's research, recorded in *Finding Faith Today* and in *Journey into Faith* (Bible Society) has established this beyond doubt.

Whilst this shift is to be welcomed, it is important to be aware of the danger of the pendulum swinging too far. In fact a process is a sustained series of events. It is important therefore not to set 'event' (in terms of moments of decision/choice) in opposition to process; but rather to see those 'crystallising moments' in the context of the wider process.

Repentance ('metanoia', in Greek, meaning to change one's mind) is foundational to entry into the Christian faith as it is to the whole way of life of the believer. However, as the faith is explained, people need to have the space and freedom to come to such 'decision moments' in their own time and way, without being pressurised. Although the process approach has a more naturally Anglican feel, it is important that the Church does not use it to avoid, where appropriate, helping people to the crisis point expressed in the baptismal question 'do you turn to Christ?'

It is important here to underline that laying the foundations for a new life orientated around faith in Christ is unlikely to happen in a five to fifteen week course. Only the desire to do so is likely to be awakened in such a limited timescale. The development of catechumenate models that create the time, space and opportunity for deepening engagement with the faith is a vital need for the second half of the Decade in the light of the very success of a number of process models of evangelism. Again, *On the Way* is a valuable resource in this task. The Roman Catholic church, with the development of the Rite of Christian Initiation of Adults, has led the way in this.

Actions Churches are taking

* *A major increase in the use of small group evangelism is taking place*

* *Supplying human interest stories for local community news sheets and local newspapers.*

QUESTIONS CHURCHES ARE ASKING

What stepping stones and space for exploring the faith are available to those wishing to enquire about the faith, and how are people likely to find their way into such groups?

How can we simplify church life so that we are more involved in the local community?

We have many bridges into the community, why is so little faith crossing either way?

Resources Churches are using

* *Church members own friendships and contact with neighbours and work colleagues*

* The Alpha Course, Christian Basics *(CPAS)*, Christians for Life *(Revd Steve Croft, St George's Ovenden, Halifax)*. *The Additional Curates Society course* Follow Me. This is our Faith *(Affirming Catholicism, Redemptionist Publications)*. How to Make Sense of God *(video produced by Housetop, London)*. Good News Down the Street *(Network Trust)*. The Key to Effective Evangelism *(Revd Barry Osborne)*

* *Courses for young people,* Just Looking *(Bible Society),* Whose life? *(CPO)*

* *Various Catechumenate courses*

* Emmaus *is a modular approach to contemporary catechumenate work, with liturgical material included, and is being published by Church House Publishing and the Bible Society in 1996*

* Hidden Treasure *is a new video resource for rural churches wanting to share their faith. It is available from the Arthur Rank Centre, Stoneleigh Park Warwickshire CV8 2LZ.*

From speaking to listening

One of the striking features of the way in which Jesus spoke to individuals was his ability to address the issue which was central to them. Rather than using an invariable formula, he spoke 'a word in season' to each person he encountered. He said one thing to Zacchaeus, another to the rich young ruler, yet another to blind

Bartimaeus, and a different 'word' again to the woman of Samaria. General statements today are much less likely to have the necessary ring of authenticity to communicate to others. This means that the Church needs to be the community which listens to the questions of those who are not members. Moreover, unless we can then speak out of our own experience we will not be likely to gain a hearing.

Evidence of this can be found in the development of 'Seeker Services', which address contemporary issues. Another expression can be found in the use of parenting courses geared to the concerns of couples (well expressed in the CPAS course entitled simply Help! I'm a Parent). The Gospel and our culture movement, from a different perspective, is also seeking to listen to what is happening in society and then address those emerging issues.

Listening is not an end in itself. Rather it is a means to an end in effective engagement with others. For some churches, listening to their communities has resulted in their engaging more fully with the pain and suffering they see. Such churches, either on their own initiative or by working with other people of goodwill, then seek to address the needs which they have found. Within this serving role, the opportunity to point to the source of the church's inspiration to action in Jesus Christ, and the opportunity to invite people to explore the Christian faith, often arise. This is not why such action in the community is undertaken, but it is a frequent fruit of it.

Clearly, evangelism is about speaking. We cannot afford to polarise speaking and listening. However, it is important that the Church begins by listening. One way of doing so is through a community/mission audit which goes beyond finding out the age and employment profile of the community and begins to probe the issue of hopes and fears. Another is by developing listening skills – for the whole of life – in all church members. To begin by listening will inevitably affect how we then go on to speak, as we must ('for we cannot help speaking about what we have seen and heard' Acts 4:20).

Actions Churches are taking

* *Running courses on creative listening*

* *Carrying out village and community appraisals with other interested groups*

* *Training people in bereavement visiting skills.*

QUESTIONS CHURCHES ARE ASKING

How can we increase our ability to listen to one another in the church?

How well do intercessions on Sunday reflect the concerns in the community and world today?

Why are we so busy and what can we do to reduce the pressure?

How can we respond better to the needs of visitors/tourists/pilgrims?

Resources Churches are using

* Country Way, *the magazine for rural churches*

* Christian Listeners *course,* and Ears to Hear *(Acorn Healing Trust)*

* Parenting courses *details from diocesan FLAME (Family Life And Marriage Enrichment) officers*

* *For churches needing to understand other faith communities before engaging in dialogue with them,* The Cross and the Crescent: responding to the challenge of Islam *is a good five session resource written by Colin Chapman and produced by Bible Society.*

From doctrine to spirituality

Whereas for many years (even centuries) the work of evangelism has been conducted within the framework of doctrine (Christian truth) opening the door to spirituality (Christian experience), it is now evident, in the image-saturated and post-modern culture in which we live, that evangelism increasingly works the other way round. Spirituality now opens the door to a grasp of Christian truth.

The Board of Mission Occasional Paper by the Revd Graham Cray, principal of Ridley Hall theological college, entitled *From Here to Where?* is a valuable introduction to the trends taking place in society and the implications for how people learn.

Evidence of this trend is seen in the great expansion of retreats, the developments of movements like Focolare, Cursillo, and the influence of movements as diverse as those centred in Taize to Toronto. This mirrors the popularity in society at large for what is called New Age teaching and practice, which majors on spirituality (sometimes leading to little or no truth content). It is also evidenced in results of surveys that regularly uncover the fact that 60% to 80% of the population pray. Grace Davie, in *Religion in Britain since 1945*, has noted the persistence of 'religious feelings' even in the context of decline in church attendance. In a survey published in *The Times* in October, 1995 when 1000 adults were questioned for BBC Radio 2's World Faith Week, two thirds of the nation believe in God but few go to church or believe that religion is important. Most said that the various Churches were out of touch with their lives and problems.

The Church has not yet grasped the full evangelistic potential of starting with spirituality, rather than doctrine, although the Cursillo movement (and its associated weekends) is a good pointer and significant model. Prayer vigils and prayer missions are, however, playing an important part in diocesan responses to the Decade.

Again, it is important that the Church does not abandon or down grade the truth content of the Christian message. True spirituality is the outworking in personal experience of the truth content of the Christian revelation. However, what is connecting with people today is the reality and outworking of faith in a person's experience, rather than the doctrine – or Church organisation. Rather like learning about computers, people are more interested in making it work than in understanding all the theory. Once they can begin to work it, they will be open to learning such theory as is likely to extend their experience.

Actions Churches are taking

* *Taking the whole PCC away for quiet days and days of prayer and reflection*

* *Running prayer schools and joining in with diocesan ones*

* *Running 'open door' parish retreats in the church building*

* *Encouraging involvement in Cursillo weekends and the Focolare movement*

* *Increasing the element of silence in services*

* *Making more of Advent, Lent and Holy Week as seasons of meditation.*

Resources churches are using

* Wild Goose Publications *(The Iona Community)*

* *Taize Community music*

* *Religious communities and retreat centres*

* Vision *magazine gives details of retreats and retreat centres.*

From gathered to dispersed

Evangelism is functioning less on the principle of 'come *here* to *hear* us' and more by way of going *there* to address *their* questions'. It is taking place increasingly outside church buildings. It is resulting in the marriage of evangelism and social action in such developments as community service projects, thrift shops, drop-in centres, and parenting courses. It is also evidenced in the significant growth of projects seeking to relate the Christian faith to every area of life, such as *The Gospel and our Culture Movement, Christians in Public Life* (CIPL), and courses such as Monday Matters (Board of Education), Sunday-Monday (CPAS), To Live and Work (MU), and Sunday-Monday (Cassells and SU).

Actions churches are taking

* *Identifying the points of influence in the community occupied by church people, not least as focus for prayer*

* *Becoming involved in Church Urban Fund projects*

* *Becoming involved in Broad Based Organising initiatives*

* *Emphasis on strategic importance of work in schools*

* *Simplifying church life to make space for dispersed activities.*

71

QUESTIONS CHURCHES ARE ASKING

How can we help church members to relate their faith to everyday life?

How can the church support the work of lay people in positions of work responsibility?

Resources churches are using

See other sections

From declaration to celebration

Whereas in the past the primary symbol of the Church's evangelism was the pulpit, today it is more likely to be the party. Certainly much evangelism is taking place in the context of meals and celebration. This was an important part of the attractiveness of many On Fire! events. In the midst of a stressed, frantic and insecure world, the opportunity to celebrate touches a deep nerve in most people. It is of course the reason, historically, why many outside the Church look to the church to assist in their own celebrations of birth, marriage and death; though the sobering comment of one teenager reminds us of the other side: 'A wedding is not really like going to church. It's a celebration.'

This connection between faith and celebration may well explain the deep instinct in many church people for events such as garden parties. The instinct is right, the forms will often have to change. Celebration is also evident in the supper and final party of the Alpha Course, and has been widely transferred, in different forms, to many different settings. The same principle characterised the Great Banquet held in the London diocese in 1995. Parties play an important part in missions too. Celebration will obviously play a vital part in the way in which the Church expresses the faith as the old millennium closes and a new millennium dawns.

One helpful principle here is to recognise that for many church members their contribution to the work of evangelism may well be in inviting others to such events. One diocesan missioner encourages people to make use of the simple formula for inviting people to special events; namely, 'I'm going, its going to be good, will you come with me?' It is obviously vital that such events really are good, well planned and professionally run, unless credibility is to be lost.

Actions churches are taking

* *Applying the Alpha supper and On Fire! celebration approach to more of church life*

* *Joining diocesan-wide feasts which have been mounted during the Decade*

* *Particularly in rural areas, developing special acts of worship related to the life of the community, such as Plough Sunday, Rogation Sunday, pets, village festivals, etc.*

QUESTIONS CHURCHES ARE ASKING

How can the church celebrate life and be a focus of celebration in the local community?

What one or two celebratory events should we be seeking to run this year? (with others?)

Resources churches are using

* *Arthur Rank Centre rural services ideas booklet*

* Country Way *magazine*

* *Listening to the community, hearing of actions by other churches.*

From the search for truth to the search for identity

This is not so much about how evangelism is being done as about what evangelism is addressing. Whereas in the past the 'proclamation of gospel truth' was addressing people's search for understanding of the world and human history and finding purpose, the focus of modern society's search can be described more appropriately as a search for identity and meaning.

Part of the Christian answer is that we do not find ourselves by looking in, in self-analysis, but by looking up to God and out to others (the two great commandments); so identity is found in community with God and others. However, the great spread of pop psychology, and personality testing methods, and indeed the growth in astrology (an occult 'personality type casting') all underline this as part of modern culture.

Actions churches are taking

* *Loving, listening to, and affirming the worth of all*

* *Developing of counselling course and ministry*

* *Involvement in and promotion of Myers-Briggs personality profiling.*

QUESTIONS CHURCHES ARE ASKING

How can we play our part in help others to discover their true identity through the knowledge of God?

How can the life of this church giving a sense of belonging, meaning and significance to all who are part of it and come into its life?

Resources churches are using

See other sections

From organists to orchestras

A significant shift is taking place in the role of the skilled individual (the 'organist' who plays one instrument that makes all other redundant) and that of the whole community (the 'orchestra'). Traditionally the work of evangelism has been seen primarily as that of the specialist preacher. There are people with such a gift, and it is important that the Church makes full use of these skills. For some, in the Decade, the number of requests to speak has been overwhelming. However, for a good number the reverse is true. This could be because the Church is doing less evangelism, but may well be better explained – as the whole of this section of the report is suggesting – by the major changes taking place in the way that evangelism is being done. Even where dioceses are training and deploying recognised evangelists, few of them are majoring on doing so from a pulpit. Again, the issue here is not either/or, but both/and.

Many of the trends noted above, such as process and celebration, cannot be done by one person. A whole team of people are required. Moreover, these operations includes a whole range of gifts from administration to hospitality, service and evangelism, teaching and pastoral care. In this way the Church demonstrates the gospel before

74

it even says anything about the truth. This trend highlights another of the findings of *Finding Faith Today*, namely that belonging proceeds believing. People may come to faith and then come to church, but much more typically they begin by making friends with a church member who shares their faith, they are then invited by that person to some event (whether primarily social or worship) which introduces them to 'a network of loving relationships', resulting in the person seeking to experience the faith which they discern gives vitality to this faith-community.

Actions churches are taking

* *Developing process approaches and celebratory events which can only happen if a team works together.*

QUESTIONS CHURCHES ARE ASKING

How can everyone play a part in the church living and telling the good news of Christ?

Resources churches are using

* *See those listed under 'process', 'listening' and 'celebration'*

* *Also, as valuable aids to developing the evangelistic work of the whole local church are two resources from the rural church which have application well beyond the rural setting, namely,* The Key to Effective Rural Evangelism, *by Barry Osborne of Sunrise ministries, and* Turning the Sod, *by Jeremy Martineau, the Rural Officer of the BOM.*

From telling to living

A further, and final, shift in the way that the Church approaches evangelism can be seen in the attention being given to how the Church is the Church. Much has been written about this in recent years, perhaps beginning with the World Council of Churches report (1968), *The Church for Others*. Lesslie Newbigin, in *The Gospel in a Pluralistic Society* addresses the need for the Church to live the gospel – especially in the chapter entitled 'the congregation as hermeneutic of the gospel'. Gerhard Linn, from Europe, in *Hear what the Spirit says to the churches*; John Drane from Scotland, in *Evangelism for a New Age*, from the United States both Loren Mead, in such books as *The Once and Future Church,* and John Westerhoff in many books including *Living the Faith Community,* and Robert Warren from England, in *Being human, being church,* have all been addressing this issue, as has Archbishop John Zizioulas, in his important theological work from the Orthodox tradition, *Being as Communion.*

These are now finding expression in projects like the CCBI learning process on missionary congregations. Certainly, in a culture which has become increasingly immune to 'truth claims', it is likely that 'truth demonstrations' in the life of local faith communities will be a vital way of communicating the faith in the coming millennium. The life of the local church needs to be prophetic through and through. As John Westerhoff puts it:

> The purpose of the Church is to manifest an alternative
> way of seeing and living life.
> *Living the Faith Community,* p.72

Again, it is important to underline that what is being said here is not that the Church should stop 'telling' and start 'living'. Such a position only takes us back to the sterile debate about whether evangelism is best done 'by lip or by life'. It has to be done by both. What is giving new insight and energy, however, is that what is to be told is the lived experience of the gospel in the faith community. This is hardly a new development, but rather a renewal of a clear biblical principle: 'you yourselves are our letter. . . known and read by everybody. . . a letter from Christ' (II Cor 3:2-3).

Actions churches are taking

* *Simplifying church life to give people more time to be active outside the church*

* *Establishing Root Groups (USPG) and Lee Abbey Household communities*

QUESTIONS CHURCHES ARE ASKING

How far does the way this church operate demonstrate the values of the kingdom of God?

How appropriate to the culture in which we are set is the way the life of this church operates?

Resources churches are using

* *In the wider work of helping churches to make the 'missionary shift' called for by Lambeth 1988, Continuing Ministerial Training (CME) officers, Adult Education Officers, and diocesan missioners, run – or know about – facilitators and courses designed to help in the missionary shift of the whole congregation.*

* The Parish Project, *is a helpful resource from the Roman Catholic church in this aspect of mission, and* Launching a Missionary Congregation, *by Robert Warren.*

QUESTIONS CHURCHES ARE ASKING

How far does the above list help to explain what is working, and what is not working, in this church's practice of evangelism?

How might the evangelism of this church be developed in the light of the trends identified above?

7

Developing the second half of the Decade

It would be tempting to come up with some simple set of priorities for the second half of the Decade to which all churches and dioceses could commit themselves; or even develop some centrally planned programme. However, vast amounts of time and energy would be needed to hammer out such a schedule; and it is doubtful whether any imposed agenda would be of a transformative nature.

The task attempted in this final section is therefore more modest. The aim is two fold.

First, under the heading of local church priorities, are five elements that seem to be vital for the renewal in mission of the local church. Second, under the title of twelve priority options a range of tasks for the whole Church (including national and diocesan resourcing and initiatives), has been identified.

Both these aspects of the way ahead have emerged out of a number of meetings and discussions with various groups, including missioners, Springboard, various networks and key people, and with a Meeting of Bishops (diocesan and suffragan) in the course of the eighteen months prior to the production of this report.

It is hoped that these two aspects will help in focusing the mind, agenda and resources of the Church in the second half of the Decade. To this end, it is intended that these lists will be considered carefully both in the local church and in diocesan, central, and voluntary agencies, with each discerning where they can best put their energies.

If the whole Church were to work from these two lists, in the second half of the Decade, it could well help in the dovetailing of creativity, skill and energy which would be most likely to prosper the work of evangelism and mission in the closing years of this millennium.

Local church mission priorities

Given that the Decade has put evangelism on the Church's agenda, and has played an important role as a catalyst to many creative initiatives, how can we best build on what has been done in the first five years? What is outlined here is a five-fold agenda for the local church for the second half of the Decade.

In view of the enormous variety of different situations and states of individual churches, no neat package can be produced to cover every situation. It is not intended that this outline should be followed in any slavish way. No doubt some churches will judge that they have already made significant strides in some areas and so will concentrate on the missing elements. Even for those churches who do not feel they have begun to engage seriously with the work of evangelism, it is important that the five elements are handled creatively according to local conditions. Certainly it would be best to major on just one or two at a time. Although there is a certain logic to the order, each church would be well advised to work with the order which best relates to its particular situation and needs. The five elements have evangelism at the centre, but are set in the wider mission context established at the start of this report.

Revitalising the spiritual life of the church. Spirituality lies at the heart of the Christian's life, and the life of the church. As noted above (see trends in evangelism), it is also the way that many in contemporary society seek to engage with the transcendent and with the religious dimension of life today. As such it is therefore crucial both to church life and to mission. By 'spirituality' is meant 'how we engage with the transcendent in life and how that shapes our living'. For the Christian this can be put in terms of 'how we encounter God and how that encounter is sustained for Christian living'.

It is this which is both the source of the individual church member's faith as well as the heart of the church's public worship. There can be no authentic evangelism unless there is a lived experience of God out of which we can speak. As *Towards the Conversion of England* put it fifty years ago, on its opening page:

> The first need in evangelism is for a strengthening and a quickening of spiritual life within the Church: we cannot separate the evangelisation of those without from the rekindling of devotion within.

The spiritual renewal of the Church must precede any evangelism that is marked by integrity and authenticity. Discovering how, to what extent and in what ways, people do actually encounter God in personal prayer and public worship is of first importance, as is work done to help people encounter God. As Gerard Hughes put it in *The God of Surprises* (p. 22):

Training in prayer should be the main preoccupation and service given by the bishops and clergy to the adult members of the church.

In particular, there is great need to ensure that public worship is seen, and experienced as, a primary means of engaging with the transcendent, with the mystery and wonder of God, and with the ultimate issues of life. The more that becomes a reality in our services, the more will others be likely to say (as in Corinth) 'God is in this place' – even if they use others words. It is the lack of that sense of what has been described as 'felt spirituality' that many occasional church attenders identify as their reason for not attending church regularly.

It is important to note that the form of spirituality will matter greatly. In a culture where 'spirituality' is perceived and practised, particularly in some expressions of the New Age movement, as anti-rational, it is important that Christian spirituality witnesses to the affirmation of the rational as well as to the value of the mystical and trans-rational. Our spirituality will need to be integrated with the mind. It will also need to be integrated with the world. The danger of some 'spiritualities' is that they are a form of, often narcissistic, withdrawal from life into the warm comfort of spiritual experience. A truly Christian spirituality will be, rather, a resource for holy living and for the pursuit of justice and peace, rather than a flight from such concerns.

Relating faith to work and daily life is the second step that needs to be taken. Too easily today faith and 'religion' are put into a separate compartment from the rest of life, when that happens then no sense can be made of the rest of life. Indeed, we have to recognise that some wish to leave life, and the problems of our world, well outside church.

However, there are a number of groups and courses that are now seeking to address this issue. Part of it will involve a clear link between intercessions on Sunday and the daily working life of the congregation. Another, perhaps more important task, is for those who preach to listen to those who actually engage with the moral dilemmas which planners in the Town Hall, doctors in the Health Service, parents in the family, and wealth creators in their working life, have to face every day. The work of Readers is a key way in which this connection between faith and life can be established, for many of them can help to establish a dialogue between the Word and the world, which is what preaching is about.

To a significant degree, the Christian faith is proclaimed not just, or primarily, by presentation of the basics of the faith, but by application of the insights of the faith to daily life. This is where we need to help in the training, support and encouragement of an articulate Church membership.

Releasing constraints to naming the Name. It has been traditional to see evangelism as something for the enthusiasts and extroverts in the Church. When they dominate the agenda, to the exclusion of other temperamental dispositions, then evangelism tends to proceed by way of constant encouragement to greater and greater evangelistic endeavours. However, there is plenty of evidence to suggest that the biggest changes often come about, not as a result of enthusing everyone to greater effort (which has its place), but rather by finding out what holds people back, and then releasing those constraints.

This is why this section is put at the mid-point in this five-fold framework; for two of the ways in which those constraints can be released are by renewing the spiritual life of the individual and local church (giving people a living story to tell), and by helping them to relate their faith to where they most frequently are in contact with non-church people.

A further reason has to do with the deep conflict in our society between the scientific culture of doubt and suspicion and the exaltation of 'facts' on the one hand, and the dimension of mystery, wonder, awe and faith on the other – which is as difficult to 'prove' as it is to deny. As Walter Wink puts it:

> Many religious people today want to hold two utterly incompatible things together: belief in God as the Creator of the world and Sovereign of the Powers, and belief in the materialistic myth of modern science, which systematically excludes God from reality.
> (*Unmasking the Powers*, p.5)

It is for this reason that the task of apologetics is so important in equipping the Church to 'give a reason for the hope that is in us' in ways that connect with the surrounding culture. The varied responses of the Church to the report of the Board for Social Responsibility on patterns of family life, *Something to Celebrate*, indicates something of the struggle that the Church is likely to have in discovering how to translate the Christian faith into an increasingly secular culture without betraying its core values.

This task of releasing the constraints to evangelism may well be an area in which the voluntary agencies will have a key role to play in producing appropriate resources.

Focusing the life of the Church around God's mission to all creation. The world around us is unlikely to be either attracted, or taken in, by a Church whose message is basically one designed to enable it to survive. The model of Christ entering this world, having laid aside his self-concerns and self-preservation, sits ill with such a Church-survival mentality. It is faithfulness to Christ, not Church survival, that is the true motivation for mission.

The understanding of mission as God's mission *(missio dei)* of love, redemption and renewal of all people, all society and all creation is one of the insights which the Church universal has grasped in recent years (see David Bosch, *Transforming Mission*, pages 389-393). It needs to be reflected in the Church's agenda. The Church, if it is not to betray its mission as Israel of the Old Testament was accused of doing, must give first priority to the coming of God's kingdom and participation in God's mission, rather than simply or primarily the growth of the Church. In a time of overstretched resources it will take the Church as much courage as Abraham, in his willingness to sacrifice his son, for the Church to give first priority to God's work in the world. We may well want to argue, as no doubt Abraham did in his mind, that the Church/son is God's chosen way of fulfilling his purposes and his promised blessing to all. Yet until the focus is God's agenda for his world, our best efforts at church growth are doomed. The three-fold groaning of Romans 8:16-26 (the groaning of creation, the believer and the Spirit) needs to shape the Church's agenda. This will involve, again, the affirmation of all those involved, through their work and voluntary actions, in the renewal of human society at whatever level – however much or little it carries a 'church' label.

QUESTIONS CHURCHES ARE ASKING

Out of the issues identified in this section, what might be the right order of priorities for this church as it seeks to develop its life and work in the second half of the Decade of Evangelism?

Reworking the life of the Church around the call to be a gospel community. Important though the work of evangelists and evangelistic events and processes are, the New Testament makes it clear that the primary instrument of mission is the Church. It is the apostolic ('sent') Church, or it is nothing. However, mission cannot be confined simply to activities the Church does outside the confines of its life; for the Church is called upon to live the gospel before it can tell the gospel to others. As such the Church is first and foremost a faith-community rather than an organisation. Though organisation is an aspect of any community, there is a fundamental difference between an organisation and a community. Community points to the value of each person as a person – whatever their contribution may or may not be. Community speaks of people held together by a common story and set of values. A community expresses those values in the way it conducts its life.

There are two particular aspects to this emphasis which need to be highlighted. One is initiation and the other is that of Church culture.

Initiation is the work of bringing people into the fullness of Christian faith and living. As the Christian world view, value system, personal identification, and lifestyle seems to recede from most people's experience of life, it becomes vital that a thorough work of initiation takes place in the lives of those who do come to faith. We must ensure that the seed we sow is of the highest quality. The joint Board of Education and Board of Mission report, *On the Way*, is a valuable contribution to this work. It is important for churches to recognise that most process approaches to evangelism do not complete the work of initiation. Full initiation is first and foremost initiation into the reign and work of God in the whole of creation and human society. The ultimate goal is more whole and fruitful human beings, not just better church members.

If the Church is the community that is living out the gospel, then how the Church is the Church is closely related to initiation. Church culture and the nature of its internal life, will need to be renewed as an expression of the gospel. Initiation introduces people to the values and lifestyle of a particular group of people. Unless that community reflects, in some measure, the gospel it proclaims to others, no initiation will bear significant fruit. The whole Church may need to be re-initiated, not in terms of rites or sacraments, but in terms of the reality of not just praying, but also living, the Lord's Prayer with its commitment of life to seek first the Kingdom of God. As Revd John Cole, diocesan missioner for Lincoln diocese has put it:

being more effectively evangelistic is not a matter of trying to learn new skills on the cheap but is a deeply costly matter of accepting God's gracious purpose and capacity in Christ to transform the whole of our lives.

The Board of Mission's Occasional Paper, *Building Missionary Congregations,* is one contribution in this area which deserves careful study and creative implementation.

Whole Church priority options

Inevitably there is some significant degree of overlap between the five-fold outline for the priorities of the local church just given, and the priority options which follow. It is important to clarify the relationship between these two sections.

Whilst local church priorities are focused on the local church and the long-term themes which it needs to engage, the list which follows is addressed to the whole Church (dioceses, national and voluntary agencies, as well as local churches). As such, each item identifies a specific piece of work which needs to be done in the second half of the Decade. As it is unlikely that much advance will be made without skills and resources for the wider church, it is to be hoped that Boards and Councils, diocesan synods and sector ministries, and voluntary agencies will all give consideration as to which of these areas calls for a specific contribution from them. If that can be done, significant advance in the work of evangelism and mission can be expected in the second half of the Decade.

Naming the Name

It has already been noted that there is much truth in the assessment that 'the Decade has got evangelism onto the Church's agenda, but it has not yet got the gospel on to the lips of church members'. Help is clearly needed to move on to that next stage in the world of evangelism. Whilst not every church member is gifted as an evangelist, all are called to bear witness to the faith and to 'give a reason for the hope that is in you'. James Lawrence of CPAS has done some helpful work in this area by running courses entitled Lost for Words, which describes where many church members start from when it comes to evangelism. The two MU courses (I Believe and Trust, and To Live and Work) are designed, at least in part, to address this issue. More work needs to be done in this area.

84

Equipping witnesses

If evangelism is concerned specifically with 'naming the Name', there is a wider task that also needs to be addressed. It is that of helping church members relate their faith to every day living in the home, workplace, neighbourhood and within social and political structures. It also includes discovering how to relate Christian insights to the various management changes and structural upheavals which many are involved in, in the worlds of education, finance, health, and social services. Courses aimed at helping people to relate their faith to daily living and the world of work are vital here (see those listed on page 71 under 'from gathered to dispersed' in the section on trends in evangelism). The Manchester diocese has being doing some pioneering work in this area of helping people to be witnesses.

Church and culture

Helping the Church to understand, and engage with, the major upheavals taking place in our society today, and discovering how to engage in the common search for a fresh set of values by which our society can hold together, are part of the work of mission. Concern for the environment is a central issue for many, especially the younger generation, that needs to be addressed. Facing real questions will often be more important than offering answers, as Martin Conway points out in his valuable Board of Mission Occasional Paper entitled, *Objectives for the Second Half of the Decade*. *The Gospel and our Culture Project*, and *Christians in Public Life*, are two such contributions. Some have sought to critique this recent emphasis on culture. This dialogue is part of the Church's learning to live and relate to a culture in profound upheaval. Often the Church's role may be no more than providing a forum in which different perspectives can enter into dialogue. Seeking the welfare of the city in which we live is part of the mission of the Church.

Missions and evangelists

These two means have, historically, been at the heart of the work of evangelism. As indicated in the section on trends in evangelism, the Church is discovering a more 'process' and 'team-work' way of sharing the faith. Yet missions and evangelists have a part to play. The work of national, diocesan and local training and recognition of evangelists remains an important part of the work of evangelism. Evangelism, not least of an itinerant nature, is a costly and lonely calling. It is to be hoped that the Church will find more effective ways of giving support to such people. Missions are all too easily considered part of 'yesterday's way of evangelism'; yet suitably re-worked they have a vital part to play. The Board of Mission hopes, in consultation with experienced missioners to draw up guide lines of best practice to enhance the value of missions well into the next millennium.

Certainly there is important work to be done in developing creative new and appropriate ways of 'doing missions'. From Franciscans to CPAS there are organisations working on just such an agenda.

Prayer and spirituality

The spiritual renewal and development of the prayer life, of both individuals and whole churches, is at the heart of the life of the Church. It is this which provides the reality in a person's knowledge of God out of which they can speak with authenticity. It is to be hoped that more dioceses will pay further attention to this, often neglected, side of the life of the Church, and that they will also consider the appointment of spirituality advisors. Work is being done by a group brought into being by the Board of Mission to help address the issues raised by seeking to articulate a church's spirituality. It is hoped to make its findings and expertise more widely available. Encouragement needs to be given to such events as Cursillo weekends and other ways in which prayer and spirituality can be enriched.

Renewing worship for mission

Although worship is not done 'for effect', it remains true that it can be a transformative event and has been the point of conversion for a number of people who now worship in our churches. Discovering how to relate worship and mission is an important part of what needs to be done in the second half of the decade. It will, hopefully, be an issue that guides the Liturgical Commission in the work of producing the ASB 2000. A wider range of expressions of such worship, from Seeker-services to The Thomas Mass are already being explored. It is important for this work be taken forward in the second half of the Decade.

Communicating the gospel to children

The agenda from the joint Board of Education and Board of Mission report, *All God's Children?*, has yet to be grasped by the Church at large. That report pointed out that with the widespread demise of the Sunday school movement, something of the order of 86% of children have no contact with the Church. Ways need urgently to be found to bridge that gap. The work of Church schools, if the opportunities are creatively and sensitively taken, is able to bring many children into touch with the Church. Through their children parents also can establish relationships with the local church. There are people working in all these areas. It may well be that more can be done to link together such people, with a view to communicating lessons about good practice to a wider circle. The Board of Education's children's officer could prove vital in this work.

Reaching youth culture

This is the other part of the *All God's Children?* agenda. It is likely to be brought to the Church's attention more fully through the report of the Board of Education, *Youth A Part,* due to be published in March 1996. Alongside work done in parishes, with the help of diocesan youth officers and their networks, more needs to be done in reaching the great number of young people with no church connections. Alternative expressions of worship are part of this.

Both the above two priorities will require the making available of major funds and staffing, which will test how far the Church is willing to invest in mission during a period of financial constraint. Retrenchment, as has already been noted, is of limited value if it does not result in funds and human resources being released for mission and development.

QUESTIONS DIOCESES, COMMITTEES AND COUNCILS NEED TO BE ASKING

Which are the top priorities out of the list in this section, and how can we set about implementing those priorities?

Initiation

The joint Board of Education, Board of Mission and Liturgical Commission report, *On the Way,* is to be welcomed as contributing to a greater understanding of the need for the church to equip those coming new into the faith and Church to live out the Gospel in the whole of their lives. Other agencies are working on further catechumenate-type resources which will take people on from the basics of the faith encounter in enquirers groups. The Catechumenate Network has been doing important work in linking together Churches and individuals working in this area. The Anglican Communion has much to learn from the Roman Catholic Church's Rite of Christian Initiation of Adults. What is now needed is a whole range of Churches, from the various traditions of the Church, to work together in a more concerted way to discover how best to bring about effective initiation – both for the health of those individuals and Churches, but also in order that those insights may be available to the whole Church.

Towards missionary congregations

Following on the paper, *Building Missionary Congregations*, there is already a considerable amount of work in hand to make the insights more widely known and available to the Church, to develop networks of churches working on the themes of this material, and to equip facilitators of churches seeking consciously to make the shift 'into mission mode'. It will be important for dioceses to recognise and give support and encouragement to these churches and networks and to make resources available.

Towards a missionary priesthood

Much of what has been said throughout this report impinges on the work of the clergy. They face a considerable range of challenges, and a fair share of discouragements too. It is important at every stage that the Church discovers the most effective way to select, train, deploy, support and give continuous ministerial training, and re-training, to the clergy. This is clearly primarily the work of ABM, but the whole Church needs to find ways of supporting and assisting in this work. Learning new skills of engaging with culture shifts, developing collaborative ministry, and becoming facilitators and liberators of laity in mission, together with training others in prayer and spirituality, and becoming permission-givers rather than permission-withholders, will require considerable demands on all concerned. Prayer and encouragement are contributions the whole Church can make in assisting in the changing role of ordained ministry.

What is said here about the ordained ministry applies in considerable measure also to the work of Readers and other authorised ministers who, with a decline in the number of ordained clergy being deployed, are playing an increasing role in the life of the Church and in forwarding the work of mission. This applies both to the public ministry of

Readers as those who lead worship and preach, but also to the pastoral work for which they are commissioned; namely, visit the sick, teaching children and young people, and catechising those new to the faith. It is a vital work that needs to be affirmed and resourced in every way possible. Equally, as stated above about clergy, help needs to be given in making adjustments to the changing of leadership in the Church.

Towards a Church in mission

In many ways all of the above items are part of a mosaic, yet the final picture needs continually to be held in mind. There is an abiding need for prophets and apologists and those who can give a vision of hope for society and for the Church's role in it. For this to happen it is important that the presuppositions of modern society and the understanding of humanity in society. Bishops Hugh Montefiore and Lesslie Newbigin, and the Revd Graham Cray, have made an important beginning in this area, but the work is far from complete. Yet without that proper critique of our contemporary culture there is unlikely to be the development of a truly prophetic word to address to today's world. Those who can enable the Church to be a Church not only rooted in the riches of its historic tradition, but also routed towards the Hope that is set before us in Christ, are vitally needed. To this end, perhaps no better understanding of the mission of the Church can be given than that outlined by Pope Paul VI on New Year's Eve, 1975, exactly twenty five years before the end of this millennium:

> We are called to be physicians of that civilisation about which we dream, the civilisation of love.

It is this end that should shape the nature of the Church's work of mission and evangelism in the second half of this Decade.

Appendix

Defining terms in Evangelisation

Paper written by Revd Donald Elliott, Secretary for the Churches' Commission on Mission (CCOM) of the Council of Churches for Britain and Ireland (CCBI) for the CCBI Conference for World Mission.

1. Mission – all God sends us to
Key bible texts: John 20:19-21, Colossians 1:19,20

Mission comprises everything that the Gospel of God's love revealed in Christ sends to the world. It embraces the pursuit of justice and peace and the care of creation, as well as the sharing of faith in personal conversation and public proclamation. Mission is concerned with the sinner and the sinned-against, the 'lost' and the 'least' of the gospels. It can involve social and political action, community and medical care, and prophetic utterance. It takes people across all kinds of frontiers and barriers, far and near, into foreign lands and alien structures. It may lead to an alliance with other people of goodwill. Its scope is ecumenical, responding to God's purpose of delivering the whole world in all its particularities from evil powers, inhuman organisations and personal brokenness, into health, liberty and unity.

2. Evangelisation – for the gospel in society
Key bible texts: Acts 1:8, Matthew 28:18-20, I Corinthians 9:19-22

Evangelisation means bringing the Gospel of Jesus Christ to people at every level of society. It is about the permeation of human relationships and cultures with Gospel values. This sometimes involves confronting the established powers with the spirituality of the Cross, and includes joining in with people's movements for justice. Evangelisation aims to create conditions for the Gospel to be considered seriously in relation to public affairs and current common sense. If the Church is the primary sign and instrument of the Gospel, then each Christian community has to be an embodiment of Gospel sharing within its particular milieu. So the renewal of church people in their calling to mission entailed in evangelisation.

3. Evangelism – awakening personal faith

Key bible texts: II Corinthians 5:15-20, Acts 8:26-38

Evangelism is about enabling personal awakening of faith in Christ among non-believers and lapsed believers. It involves sharing faith person to person. The aim is to provide everyone with the opportunity to respond freely to the Gospel of God's love within their own setting. This includes the possibility of a definite commitment to the community of faith – the Church. Dialogue – but also sometimes confrontation – will be involved.

4. The three are linked

Evangelism cannot proceed from any base other than an evangelising community that is seeking to live out the Gospel. An evangelising Church has, by reason of the internal dictates of the Gospel, to be committed to the whole mission of God. 'The medium is the message'.

For the love of God impels us to desire that the people of the world be saved from the destructive forces both within themselves and in the way things are organised. So the love of God must be made plain personally and publicly by deed and word, and people encouraged to consider joining those who feel impelled thus to embody and share the Gospel.

The mission has to be 'in Christ's way', without coercion or disregard of persons or cultures. Personal conversion and social transformation are the work of the Holy Spirit.